# COMPUTATIONAL INTELLIGENCE IN SOFTWARE QUALITY ASSURANCE

# SERIES IN MACHINE PERCEPTION AND ARTIFICIAL INTELLIGENCE*

*Editors:* **H. Bunke** (Univ. Bern, Switzerland)
**P. S. P. Wang** (Northeastern Univ., USA)

---

*For the complete list of titles in this series, please write to the Publisher.

Series in Machine Perception and Artificial Intelligence – Vol. 63

# COMPUTATIONAL INTELLIGENCE IN SOFTWARE QUALITY ASSURANCE

## S. Dick

*University of Alberta, Canada*

## A. Kandel

*University of South Florida, USA*

**World Scientific**

NEW JERSEY • LONDON • SINGAPORE • BEIJING • SHANGHAI • HONG KONG • TAIPEI • CHENNAI

*Published by*

World Scientific Publishing Co. Pte. Ltd.

5 Toh Tuck Link, Singapore 596224

*USA office:* 27 Warren Street, Suite 401-402, Hackensack, NJ 07601

*UK office:* 57 Shelton Street, Covent Garden, London WC2H 9HE

**British Library Cataloguing-in-Publication Data**
A catalogue record for this book is available from the British Library.

COMPUTATIONAL INTELLIGENCE IN SOFTWARE QUALITY ASSURANCE
Series in Machine Perception and Artificial Intelligence — Vol. 63

ISBN 981-256-172-2

Printed in Singapore by World Scientific Printers (S) Pte Ltd

**Dedication**

This book is dedicated to my parents and family, for their unstinting love and support; to my friends and colleagues, for their inspiration; and most important, to my dearest wife Ashling, the love of my life.

## Acknowledgements

I would like to thank Dr. Abraham Kandel, for his support and advice over the past several years, and Drs. Horst Bunke, Dewey Rundus, Kenneth Christensen, Carlos Smith and Mark Last for their valuable advice. My thanks also to Dr. Vairavan of the University of Wisconsin-Milwaukee for providing the datasets used in Chapters 4 and 5. Last but not least, my thanks to my editor, Ian Seldrup, for his patience and support through all the difficulties of bringing this book to press. The writing of this book was supported in part by the Natural Sciences and Engineering Research Council of Canada under grant nos. PGSB222631-1999 and G230000109, and in part by the National Institute for Systems Test and Productivity at USF under the USA Space and Naval Warfare Systems Command grant no. N00039-01-1-2248.

# Foreword

Undoubtedly, Software Engineering is concerned with the most complex and abstract systems ever designed by humans. The rapidly growing and widespread presence and profound complexity of software systems brings to the picture fundamental concepts of software quality including such key components as reliability, portability and maintenance, just to allude to only a few of them. Software processes and software development are profoundly human – driven. The human factors are omnipresent throughout the entire software development process starting from the requirement analysis, moving to general architectural considerations, design, implementation, and ending up with software validation and verification. Given the two important aspects of complexity and human centricity, modeling software processes and software quality becomes a genuine challenge. On one hand, we envision a broad spectrum of models and specific modeling techniques quite often brought into Software Engineering from other disciplines (e.g., system reliability) that dwell upon the fundamental techniques of multivariate linear and nonlinear regression analysis. On the other hand, by being aware of the human-based and human-centric software processes, there is a growing interest in other alternative methodological approaches to system modeling. One of them has emerged within the framework of Computational Intelligence (CI). Interestingly, the models of CI exhibit a number of features that are of paramount interest and high practical relevance to Software Engineering. The CI-based models can be formed on a basis of heterogeneous data (including experimental data and quite subjective expert feedback). The CI constructs are also inherently transparent (owing to their logic underpinnings) and highly modular. The mechanisms of evolutionary optimization coming as an integral part of the overall CI platform are of high relevance when dealing with the structural and parametric optimization of such models.

Being fully cognizant of the complexity of the endeavor, this research monograph, authored by Professors Scott Dick and Abraham Kandel, ventures into the fundamentals of software quality assurance. Here, this very idea of software quality assurance has been challenged and significantly augmented in the setting of Computational Intelligence. A significant part of the book focuses on software reliability – an important and highly visible feature of most software products. The fundamental principles of modeling software reliability are formed in the language of fractals instead of stochastic or probabilistic models. This offers a new and attractive view at the essence of this software quality. The authors put forward several quite compelling arguments and augment them by carefully organized and coherent experimental evidence. The ideas of understanding software measures (metrics) presented in the realm of unsupervised learning, notably fuzzy clustering, are highly relevant. Revealing the structure in software data helps shed light on possible categories of software modules, identifying those components that might deserve more attention and generating some recommendations as to their stability are of vital interest to software developers, testers, and software managers. With regard to software metrics and categories of software modules, the authors emphasize an importance and possible implications of heavily skewed software data and discuss various ways of dealing with this aspect of software modeling.

The material is covered in a highly authoritative fashion and the presentation of the key ideas is systematic, well motivated and will appeal to any reader. While the authors managed to cover a vast and quite unexplored territory (and with this regard the presented material is highly informative), the reading of the book could be very much inspiring. What are the fundamentals and practical implications of fractal analysis of software phenomena? What would be the most beneficial hybridization of fuzzy sets, neural networks and evolutionary optimization when being applied to problems of software development, reliability, maintenance, and software quality? What type of data should we collect and how could we treat the prescriptive and descriptive facets of software modeling? The book provides the reader not only with some useful insights but what is just as important, stimulates further investigations and detailed pursuits in this direction.

Professors Dick and Kandel deserve our sincere appreciation and thanks by bringing to the research community such a timely and important volume. This monograph definitely opens new avenues, answers intriguing questions and delivers strong experimental evidence. Undeniably, the book will be greatly appreciated by the community of Quantitative Software Engineering and Computational Intelligence.

Witold Pedrycz

February 8, 2005

# Preface

Software systems are at once the most complex and the least reliable technological systems human beings construct. A large software system can have over $10^{20}$ states, and the reliability of software is infamously poor. Software engineers must usually make assertions about the reliability of software systems after having observed only an insignificant fraction of the possible states of the system. New mechanisms and techniques for inferring the overall quality and reliability of software systems are needed. In this book, we will describe three investigations into the use of computational intelligence and machine learning for software quality assurance, which lead toward such mechanisms.

Our first contribution is the use of chaos theory for software reliability modeling. Software reliability growth models (SRGM) are used to gauge the current and future reliability of a software system. Virtually all current SRGMs assume that software failures occur randomly in time, an assumption that has never been experimentally tested despite being criticized by a number of authors in the field. We have used nonlinear time series analysis to ascertain whether software reliability data from three commercial software projects come from a stochastic process, or from a nonlinear deterministic process. Evidence of deterministic behavior was found in these datasets, lending support to the idea that software failures may be *irregular* in nature. This is a qualitatively different form of uncertainty than randomness, one that is best modeled using the techniques of fractal sets and chaos theory rather than probability theory.

Our second contribution is the use of fuzzy clustering and data mining in software metrics datasets. Software metrics are measures of source code, which are intended as a basis for software quality improvement. Literally hundreds of metrics have been published in the literature, but no generally applicable regression model relating metrics and failure rates has been found. Instead of statistical regression, we use unsupervised machine learning, in the form of the fuzzy c-means algorithm, to analyze three collections of software metrics from commercial systems. This investigation highlights additional challenges for machine learning in the software metrics domain, one of which is skewness. The most common machine learning approach to overcoming skewness is to resample the dataset; however, this has never been attempted in the software metrics domain. Hence, our third contribution is the use of resampling algorithms to calibrate a decision tree to preferentially recognize high-risk classes of modules. We consider how the calibration process, as well as the operational decision tree, can be woven into an iterative software development process.

This book will primarily be of interest to researchers in the areas of computational intelligence or software engineering, and particularly those interested in interdisciplinary research between those two fields. It will also be suitable for use as a textbook in an advanced graduate class in either field, or to practicing software engineers interested in how computationally intelligent technologies may be used to aid their work. The original research material in this book is supported by an extensive review of both software engineering and computational intelligence, covering over 300 references.

Scott Dick
Abraham Kandel

February 2005

# Contents

# Chapter 1

# Software Engineering and Artificial Intelligence

## 1.1 Introduction

A \$500 million dollar rocket self-destructs because of an arithmetic overflow [169]. A radiation therapy machine kills patients instead of helping them [26]. Software systems permeate every corner of modern life, and any failure of those systems impacts us. Sometimes the effect is trivial – just the time required to restart a program. In other cases, life, limb or property could be in jeopardy. One of the primary goals of software testing is to quantify the reliability of a software system, and to ensure that the system's failure modes do not include catastrophic consequences to people or property. As the Ariane-5 and Therac-25 incidents showed, that goal has not yet been achieved, despite the enormous resources invested in software development. The USA Department of Defense spends \$42 billion dollars per year developing and maintaining computer systems and only \$7 billion of this goes to hardware [30]. The problem is that software systems are so complex – $10^{20}$ states or more in a large system [84] – that software engineers are not currently able to test software well enough to insure its correct operation. Exhaustive testing is obviously impossible, and to date no one has found a way to conduct non-exhaustive testing that provides assurance that a software system will perform as intended. The problem we address is finding mechanisms or relationships to more accurately determine the quality of software systems, without visiting a large fraction of their possible states. Novel ways of using nonlinear time

1

series analysis and data mining to model software reliability and quality will be investigated. These investigations point the way towards using intelligent technologies to support human developers in creating software systems by exploiting the different forms of uncertainty present in a software system.

For a number of years, researchers have been trying to use artificial intelligence (AI) techniques to automate the software engineering and testing process [1, 6, 9, 11, 31, 42, 49, 57, 60, 75, 99, 129, 131, 173, 204, 213, 219, 269, 270, 273, 281, 282, 292]. The goal is to let a computer perform much of the repetitive work involved in creating and testing software. A computer that can interpret a high-level description of a problem into working software would remove fallible humans from the business of coding, while a system that is able to choose its own test cases can generate and run tests far faster than a human being. If the computer also somehow understood the nature of software failures, then it could use that information to automatically generate better test cases. Needless to say, these goals remain elusive. However, there has been a significant amount of work done in using AI for various aspects of software development and testing. Various kinds of expert systems have been proposed to examine software metrics and help guide developers [47, 67, 68, 93, 95, 133, 138, 139, 140, 143, 266]. AI algorithms have been investigated for generating test cases [89, 179, 259]. Perhaps the most ambitious effort was the research in automatic programming, which attempted to create an AI system that could autonomously write new programs [1, 9, 11, 31, 75, 99, 129, 269, 273, 292].

Of particular interest in the present study is the use of computational intelligence in software development and testing. Computational intelligence (CI) is the name given to a synergistic group of technologies that exploit a tolerance for uncertainty and incomplete or imprecise data, in order to model complex systems and support decision making in uncertain environments. A key characteristic of CI technologies is that they embody different, but complementary, avenues of attack for system modeling and decision support under uncertain conditions [90]. Neural networks, genetic algorithms, evolutionary computation, fuzzy logic, rough sets, fractals and chaos theory, and all the various hybridizations of these technologies fall under the rubric of computational intelligence.

Since the software development and testing environment is fraught with incomplete and imprecise information, along with a variety of forms and sources of uncertainty, CI technologies are excellent candidates for modeling software processes and products. CI technologies are also closely related to case-based reasoning, machine learning, and data mining algorithms, all of which deal with system modeling or decision making in real-world, uncertain environments, and which have been used for modeling software products and processes. The largest body of work in this area is the use of CI technologies to predict software quality from software metrics [7, 8, 47, 67, 68, 93, 95, 133, 138, 139, 140, 141, 143, 190, 266]; there has also been significant work done in using CI technologies for software cost estimation [22, 77, 94, 233, 272], and in the computationally intelligent generation of test cases [192, 193, 225, 284, 285].

We present three specific contributions towards the use of intelligent systems in software engineering. The first contribution is in using chaos theory for software reliability modeling. Software reliability growth models (SRGM) are used to gauge the current and future reliability of a software system. Virtually all current SRGM are based on stochastic processes, and incorporate the assumption that software failures occur randomly in time, an assumption that has never been experimentally tested. Software failures, however, ultimately arise from mistakes in the program's source code, mistakes that are made by human beings. Human mistakes in general do not appear to be random events; more specifically, there is no probability distribution that has been shown to govern when a programmer will make an error. Instead, the infrequent and unpredictable occurrence of human errors seems to more closely resemble the form of uncertainty known as irregularity. Irregularity is properly modeled by chaos theory and fractal sets, in the same way that randomness is properly modeled by probability theory. Accordingly, nonlinear time series analysis is used to ascertain whether software reliability data comes from a stochastic process, or if the data in fact arise from a nonlinear deterministic process. Reliability growth data drawn from three commercial software systems was examined; these datasets do indeed exhibit the signatures of deterministic behavior, and hint at chaotic behavior. This experimental evidence shows that nonlinear deterministic models are a sound alternative to stochastic processes in software reliability growth modeling.

The second contribution is the use of fuzzy clustering and data mining in software metrics datasets. Software metrics are measures of source code, which are intended as a basis for software quality improvement. Literally hundreds of metrics have been published in the literature, each of which quantifies some aspect of a program. These metrics do seem to be related to the number of failures a module will suffer, in that the correlation between metrics and failure rates is quite strong. However, no one has discovered a generally applicable regression model relating metrics and failure rates. Thus, while a relationship clearly exists between software metrics and quality, no one knows precisely what this relationship is. As an alternative to statistical regression, some authors have investigated the use of machine learning and data mining to search for relationships between software metrics and software quality. In general, the techniques that have been used are supervised learning algorithms such as neural networks or decision trees. However, unsupervised learning actually appears to be a better fit to the software engineering process than supervised learning. Accordingly, the fuzzy c-means clustering algorithm was employed to explore three datasets of software metrics in a fuzzy cluster analysis. These datasets were collected from commercial software systems in the late '80s and early '90s. This cluster analysis is the first time that the fuzzy c-means algorithm has been applied to software metrics data, and revealed additional characteristics of this application domain that pose a special challenge for machine learning algorithms.

One of the challenges we highlight for machine learning in software metrics is skewness. In general, any collection of software metrics will be skewed towards modules with low metric values and low failure rates. Skewness has a deleterious effect on machine learning, because machine learning algorithms will try to optimize a global performance measure over an entire dataset. A minority class will thus receive less attention, and the machine learner will be less capable of recognizing minority class examples. This is a common problem in machine learning, and it is solved by resampling the dataset, in order to *homogenize* the class distribution. Resampling has not previously been investigated in the software metrics domain; the only attempt to deal with skewness was the use of differing misclassification penalties in a decision tree [139]. Our third contribution is an investigation of resampling as a way to focus a machine learner's attention on modules that pose a high development risk. Undersampling was used to thin out the majority classes from the three metrics datasets, along with oversampling to build up the minority classes. In this manner, a decision tree classifier was trained to preferentially recognize high-risk modules in the three datasets, even though these are a minority of the overall dataset. This research could be used in an iterative software engineering process to create an automated filter that recognizes potentially troublesome modules. This filter would be a significant improvement over existing systems because a calibrated decision tree will reflect the context of a specific project, rather than being a generic set of rules with little relevance to the current project.

In the remainder of this chapter, key concepts from the existing literature on software engineering, AI, and Computational Intelligence are reviewed. This review continues in Chapter 2, where the focus is on software testing and how it can be enhanced through the use of AI and Computational Intelligence. The software reliability investigation is presented in Chapter 3, and the fuzzy clustering experiments in Chapter 4. Chapter 5 is devoted to an investigation of how resampling might be used in software engineering datasets; the chapter closes with a discussion of how Computational Intelligence might be directly used in a software development process. We conclude with a summary of our contributions and a discussion of future work in Chapter 6.

## 1.2 Overview of Software Engineering

Software engineering is at once similar to all other engineering disciplines, and radically different from any of them. It is similar in that a complex artifact must be created by a developer in order to meet the needs of a client; it is different in that the end product is not a physical construct, but a *logical* one. Software systems have a life cycle like any other engineering artifact; they are conceived, designed, built, and operated, but they do not age or wear out. An unaltered piece of software remains exactly as capable of fulfilling its original mission, in its original environment, even thirty or forty years later as it was the day it was installed. Software undergoes design changes and maintenance like any other system; however, due to its logical nature, software seems absurdly easy to change. There is a huge temptation to add features and perform wholesale alterations, because they seem so effortless. The price is that bugs will be added as well, ultimately degrading the quality of the whole software system.

### *1.2.1 The Capability Maturity Model*

Clearly, there must be some organized process for creating software. The task of creating software is hugely complex; the work of literally hundreds or thousands of programmers must coordinate to produce a large software system, and *each one* of those programmers must play some small creative role in developing the system. Even junior programmers assigned to code a thoroughly planned design contribute the creativity of their own implementation strategy. Moreover, each project is unique, and an organization's development process must be tailored to the particular software system under construction [232]. Thus, a natural starting point for a review of software engineering is to look at how organizations can establish and improve their own software development process – whatever it may be – in the context of the Capability Maturity Model.

The Software Engineering Institute at Carnegie-Mellon University developed the Capability Maturity Model (CMM), which rates how effective an organization is at the software development task and helps guide organizations to improve their processes [227]. The CMM begins by rating organizations as belonging to one of five categories: *initial, repeatable, defined, managed,* and *optimizing.* Organizations at the *initial* level have no project management structure at all. All development projects use an ad-hoc organization, and any successes are the result of individual heroics. Organizations at the *repeatable* level employ a basic project management structure that at least tracks software cost, function, and schedule, permitting earlier success on similar projects to be repeated. Those at the *defined* level have a complete project management and project engineering framework in place. Each development project uses these frameworks, customized as necessary. *Managed* organizations employ a basic quality-control scheme. Software quality is measured at various points in the development cycle, and any flaws thus uncovered are corrected. Finally, the *optimizing* organizations are continually measuring and improving their development processes, while exploring the opportunities offered by novel technologies. A 2001 self-assessment survey attempted to gauge how mature the overall software industry is. More than a quarter of the organizations surveyed (27.1%) reported that they were at the *initial* level. The largest group, 39.1%, was at the *repeatable* level, and 23.4% felt that they had reached the *defined* level. Only 10.4% reported that they believed they were at the *managed* or *optimizing* levels [34].

Besides simply ranking organizations, the CMM provides guidance on how organizations can improve. At each level, the CMM identifies a set of core competencies, and these competencies represent a path to organizational improvement. Successive CMM levels lead organizations through a learning process that, hopefully, results in the organization being an efficient, effective software development group. One point of particular significance is that the CMM is designed to be a step-by-step guide for improving over time; an organization does not become a CMM-*optimizing* development group by simply throwing the specified tasks into their development process. The different stages of the CMM are designed to enhance organizational discipline, not to be a checklist [227]. The CMM is a high-level description of how organizations can improve their software processes, with the implication being that this will lead to improved software products. Our focus, however, is analyzing and improving software *products,* the actual deliverables for a client. Accordingly, the development of software products, rather than the refinement of processes, is the focus of the remainder of this review.

### *1.2.2 Software Life Cycle Models*

Software systems are conceived, built, operated, and finally replaced when they are no longer useful. However, no one is yet certain what the *exact* life cycle of a software system should be. The first widely accepted proposal was the waterfall model [254], which is the typical life cycle of other engineering products, adapted for the use of software developers (see Fig. 1.1). The waterfall model, an expansion of the staged model [17], describes the evolution of a software system from the initial collection of user requirements through the retirement of the system, as shown in Figure 1.1. This particular version involves eight phases, all of which are essential to any software life cycle: a feasibility study, requirements specification, design, implementation, testing, installation & acceptance, operation & maintenance, and finally retirement.

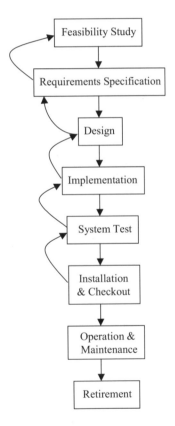

Figure 1.1: Waterfall Life-Cycle [232]

The first step in a software development project under the waterfall model is to determine whether continuing the project at all is a useful idea. The developers have to decide if they can deliver the software product on time and on budget. A two-person shop, for instance, should not take on the next upgrade of the Solaris™ operating system. Assuming that the project is feasible, the actual work of producing a software system begins with the collection of user requirements. Once a complete picture of the user's needs has been formed, the requirements will usually be formalized as a requirements specification. This is the definitive statement of what the software will do, and all subsequent work is directed towards fulfilling the specification. A software architecture and detailed design are worked out during the design stage, and then translated into working computer code in the implementation stage. The completed system is then tested, and upon passing its tests, is released to the end users, who must install it and perform any acceptance tests. The system then enters regular service. Over time, bugs will be corrected and new capabilities added to the software; these are considered maintenance activities. Finally, the software will be retired when it becomes more economical to purchase a new software system of superior functionality [40, 232].

The waterfall model as used today incorporates the ability to backtrack by one stage in order to fix a flaw in the system under development. That, however, is the limit to which the waterfall model can support incremental development. Thirty years' worth of industry experience now shows that this waterfall model is seriously flawed, and that incremental or evolutionary life cycles are far more appropriate for software development [232]. However, it is interesting to note that the seminal papers on the waterfall model [254], and the SAGE development model that preceded it [17], both described the development of a *pilot* system as an essential activity (the fact that the SAGE system used a pilot system was discussed in a forward to the ICSE'87 reprint). The waterfall model, as it is employed today, does not incorporate the development of a pilot system, and few developers attempt them.

The prototyping [160], evolutionary [41] and incremental development lifecycles [232] were developed to more closely match the reality of software development. The evolutionary model is a high-level analysis of changes that occur during the lifetime of a software system. The emphasis is on a view of software evolution as a complex feedback loop with significant nonlinearities and delays. The prototyping and incremental lifecycles are iterative in nature; each version of the system becomes the basis for the next, with a relatively short turnaround time. The incremental development model is depicted in Figure 1.2.

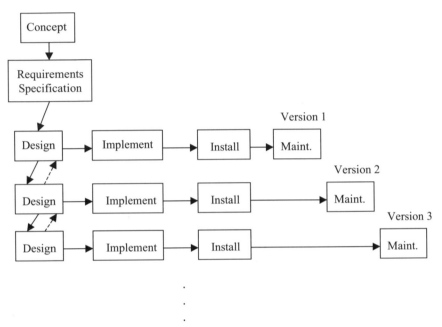

Figure 1.2: Incremental Life-Cycle [232]

The Fountain model [239] was proposed for software systems that have a strongly iterative life cycle. As its name implies, the basic metaphor of the fountain is used, in which water is shot out of a nozzle, and then falls back into a pool. In the fountain model (Figure 1.3), the project rises through the different phases of software development, often falling back one or more phases. Finally, when the project is complete, it exits the fountain into the operation and maintenance phase. As with other iterative models, the main criticism leveled at the Fountain model is that it does not support clear tracking of project milestones, thus making project scheduling difficult [239].

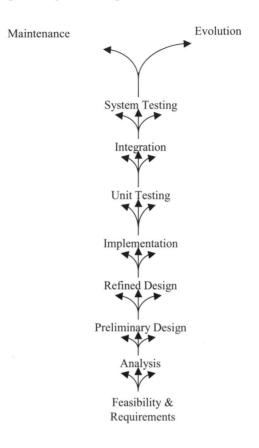

Figure 1.3: Fountain Life-Cycle [239]

The Spiral model proposed by Boehm [23] combines the strengths of both the waterfall and incremental life cycles. The Spiral model is iterative, with the transition between each iteration controlled by a formal risk assessment. In this model, the emphasis is on controlling system risks by identifying and mitigating them. A cycle begins by determining what alternatives are available, including in-house development or commercial off-the-shelf software. A risk analysis is conducted, and prototypes developed. The current iteration of the system is then designed, implemented, and tested, and then planning begins for the next cycle. The Spiral model is depicted in Figure 1.4.

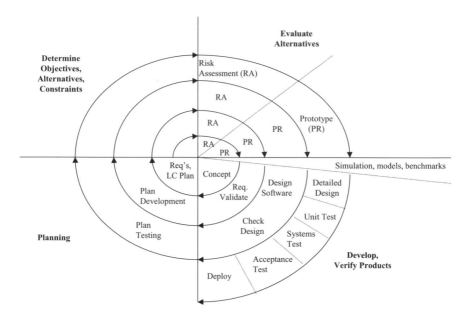

Figure 1.4: Spiral Life-Cycle [23]

### 1.2.3 Modern Software Development

In the past thirty years, software engineering as a profession has undergone several revolutionary changes, as engineers have sought "the right way" to create reliable, useful software systems. The days when a single engineer could write his own operating system or applications are long since gone; they passed away in the 1950s, when computers became powerful enough to run large-scale programs (of which SAGE was an early example [17]). Since that time, the technology deployed to assist human software developers has been critically important. The invention of the automatic compiler, taken for granted today, is a dramatic example. In 1956 the SAGE team had to build their own compiler; today, building a compiler is a standard term project for computer science students. Other technologies have not stood the test of time; structured development, data-oriented design and information engineering were widely hailed in their time as mechanisms to improve software quality, just as object-oriented programming is today [40]. There are already competing technologies, such as aspect-oriented programming [197], seeking to displace or significantly alter the object-oriented model. In this section, some modern methods in software engineering are reviewed, including requirements engineering, software architectures, object-oriented design, design patterns, and the conduct of software maintenance.

### 1.2.3.1 Requirements Engineering

A professional software engineer is an expert in transforming a stated set of requirements into a working software system. A software engineer is most emphatically *not* an expert in virtually any of the application domains he or she will be called on to design software systems for. Likewise, the clients (or their experts) are well schooled in the application domain, but generally have no experience in developing large-scale software systems. The gap between software expertise and domain expertise can manifest itself in subtle ways, and can be very, very dangerous [6]. For this reason, a complete and consistent set of requirements is a vital part of every software development project. These requirements must completely cover the functional, behavioral and non-behavioral aspects of a software system. *Functional* aspects include all the required operations that the software is expected to perform, or services it is expected to provide. *Behavioral* aspects include all of the sequencing and possible overlapping of system functions – essentially the flow of control within the software system. Finally, *non-behavioral* aspects of software are those attributes that do not belong to the previous two categories, such as reliability, usability, scalability, etc. [232]

*Requirements engineering* is the name given to a structured, exhaustive elicitation of requirements for a software system, and it is a vital part (perhaps *the* most vital part) of a software project. The principle products of a requirements engineering activity are a software requirements specification and a quality assurance plan. A software requirements specification describes the functional, behavioral and non-behavioral attributes of a system, and also provides a context for the project. The USA Department of Defense also requires traceability for all requirements (DOD standard DI-MCCR-80025A), which means that each requirement in the specification can be mapped back to a specific user need. The quality assurance plan specifies the quality criteria, how they are to be tested, cost constraints, and the system acceptance criteria [232]. In the remainder of this section, only the generation of a software requirements specification will be discussed.

Requirements engineering begins by determining the context of a software system: its environment, the items it is expected to help produce, the principal functions of the software system, and the system's modes of operation. From this context, we determine the system functionality, external interfaces, performance requirements, constraints, and required attributes, which form the core of the software requirements specification (see Figure 1.5). With these global considerations in place, we can proceed to analyze specific requirements. As a minimum, every input to the system and every system output (the observable behavior) must be described, along with the non-behavioral attributes of the system. There are a number of ways to specify the observable behavior of a system; object-oriented analysis, Jackson System Development, finite state machines and Petri nets are just a few [232]. Formal specification methods are one important class of techniques for specifying observable behavior; we will discuss these next.

Formal specifications provide a mathematically sound basis for program development. They are rigorous mathematical descriptions of system behavior, and are the basis for a proof of program correctness. They are essential tools in safety-critical systems, because only a mathematical proof of correctness can insure that there will not be a dangerous or catastrophic system failure. Formal specifications are now widely used even in systems that are not safety-critical, in order to meet ISO 9000 certification criteria. Some of the formal methods used in the software industry include Petri nets, the Vienna Development Method, Z notation, and the Cleanroom Black Box method.

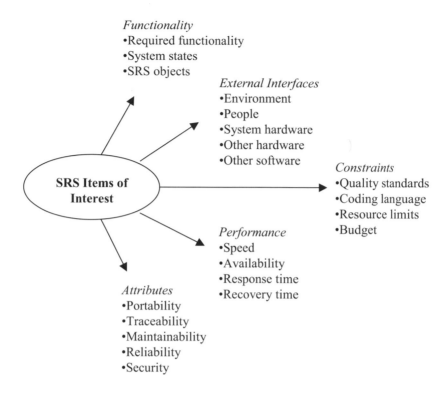

*Functionality*
•Required functionality
•System states
•SRS objects

*External Interfaces*
•Environment
•People
•System hardware
•Other hardware
•Other software

*Constraints*
•Quality standards
•Coding language
•Resource limits
•Budget

**SRS Items of Interest**

*Performance*
•Speed
•Availability
•Response time
•Recovery time

*Attributes*
•Portability
•Traceability
•Maintainability
•Reliability
•Security

Figure 1.5: Software Requirements Specification Issues [232]

Petri nets are one of the oldest formal specification methods currently in use [232]. They are used to model concurrent systems and systems that involve asynchronous communication. A Petri net is a form of finite state machine in which a number of state transitions can take place concurrently. Each transition is associated with input and output storage locations (places), and there are a number of tokens circulating within the net. All transitions fire at the same time; a transition can fire if and only if each input place for that transition is holding a token. When a transition fires, a token is removed from each input place associated with that transition, and one is added to each output place for that transition. Petri nets can be analyzed for several properties, such as liveness, safety, boundedness, and reachability [232]. An introduction to Petri nets may be found in [234].

The Vienna Development Method (VDM) [21] was created at IBM's Vienna Laboratory. In VDM, all modules in a program are treated as mathematical functions mapping inputs to outputs. A VDM specification requires that all assumptions about input arguments (preconditions) and results (postconditions) be formally described in mathematical notation. The most important aspect of a VDM specification is the *proof obligation*, which is a relation or set of relations that must hold between inputs and results. An implementation of a module must be shown to satisfy the proof obligation in its specifications [232]. More on VDM specifications may be found in [120].

Z specifications are built up of schemas, which are a structured description of both the static and dynamic features of a process. The static features of a process are its inputs, outputs, and the function prototype of any operations that the process needs to carry out, which are represented as declarations. The dynamic features of a process are represented by preconditions and postconditions, using the operations of elementary set theory as well as input and output operators. See [271] for further reading [232]. Finally, the Cleanroom Black Box method treats a module as a black box, and simply specifies the module's response to inputs, providing that a given set of constraints is satisfied. The dynamics of the module are represented via production rules [232].

## 1.2.3.2 Software Architecture

The term *software architecture* refers to the global structuring of a software system. It is a definition of how the overall system will operate, rather than a detailed module design. According to the *IBM Systems Journal*, "the term *architecture* is used… to describe the attributes of a system as seen by the programmer, i.e., the conceptual structure and functional behavior, as distinct from the organization of the data flow and controls, the logical design, and the physical implementation," [232]. Brooks has cited architectural integrity as a key component of software quality [29], and Goel identified the breakdown of architectural integrity through maintenance errors as the principal cause of "aging" in software systems [87].

An architecture should be flexible, extensible, portable and reusable. A flexible architecture is one that permits changes with minimal disruption, and allows external interfaces and timing constraints to change easily. Extensible architectures allow new functionality to be added without the need for extensive changes, such as when adding additional devices to a bus. A portable system runs on different platforms without significant change. A system that can be compiled and run on both Microsoft Windows™ and Sun Microsystems' Solaris™, for instance, is portable between those two platforms. The Java language and the ANSI C standard were created to ensure that programs only had to be written once, and could then be recompiled for any desired target machine. Reusability is a software characteristic that is supported by an architectural design. A software component is reusable if it can be removed from the application it was written for, inserted into another, and still perform its original task [232].

There are several architectural styles in wide use in software engineering. Each style has application areas it is particularly well suited for. The data flow, call & return, independent process, virtual machine and repository architectures can be employed in a wide variety of application domains. There are also domain-specific architectures, which are not so useful outside of their original application domain. Architectural choices are extremely important; the software architecture is one of the main constraints on software evolution [160].

Data flow architectures operate on some continuous stream of input data. The system accepts an input, processes it, outputs a result, and immediately moves on to the next input. Batch job control systems are an early example of this architecture, as are process controllers and cryptographic systems. Process controllers are used in plants to automatically regulate some process (chemical reaction, manufacturing, etc). They are placed in a feedback loop with the plant, and regulate the plant according to a specified control law. Cryptographic systems take a stream of ordinary text, and encrypt it so that it is unreadable. This ciphertext is then sent to a recipient, who alone can decrypt the ciphertext stream back into plaintext [232].

The call & return architecture will be the most familiar to a beginning programmer. Call & return architectures arrange components in a driver-worker relationship, such as a C main program and worker functions. Object-oriented architectures, layered architectures, and any other architecture that uses a master-slave relationship among its components are considered call & return systems [232].

Independent process architectures are software systems composed of autonomous processes, which may or may not communicate with each other. Distributed and parallel systems are good examples of this kind of architecture. The communicating process model [107] specifies that processes communicate through *ports*, over unidirectional *channels*. The pattern of channels between processes can be manipulated to provide any desired configuration, each of which is its own architecture. Agent architectures are another form of independent process architecture, one that is receiving considerable attention today. An agent is a persistent, autonomous software entity that exists for a specific purpose. An agent has its own input/output ports, memory, and processing capabilities. These are enormously varied, since agents perform a number of tasks. One of the more popularized types of agent architecture is the intelligent agent, which will directly interact with a user in its input and output channels [232].

A virtual machine architecture is, in essence, a simulator. The idea is to present user programs with a specific target machine architecture, independently of the processor the software actually runs on. This is a step beyond portability; instead of simply enforcing a standard language that can be recompiled for a target system, a virtual machine allows programs to run without *any* changes or recompilation. The best-known virtual machine today is probably the Java Virtual Machine (JVM), which simulates a processor who native assembly language is Java [168]. Other examples include the Adaptive Intelligent System architecture [100].

Repository architectures are another enormously important architectural style. This type of architecture includes database systems, along with reuse libraries, hypertext systems such as the World Wide Web, archival systems and blackboards. Database systems in particular are widely deployed in a variety of industries, and are the focus of almost every corporate Information Technology department. Repository architectures consist of a data store, a central record of the system state, and independent components implementing the functionality of the system. These independent components will normally access the data store and update the central state information in the course of their activities [232].

### 1.2.3.3 OO Design

The procedure-oriented design paradigm is essentially structured programming, combined with either top-down or bottom-up decomposition of a system into modules [48]. One problem with this design paradigm is that it appears to reach its limits in program with more than 100,000 lines of source code [211]. Procedural systems larger than this approximate value seem to be much less reliable. Object-oriented systems can be much larger than procedure-oriented systems, without encountering the same drop-off in reliability at 100,000 lines of code that seems to affect procedural systems [211].

Object-oriented design is based on the principles of encapsulation, inheritance, and polymorphism. Encapsulation means that data, and the operations on it, are treated as a single, indivisible unit, known as an object. The operations and data within an object are collectively known as the attributes of that object, while the operations by themselves are known as methods. The data within an object can only be accessed by using that object's methods. This supports the design principle of information hiding, which asserts that users of a program unit should only have access to the external interface of that unit, and not its internal data and organization [211, 275].

Inheritance is the ability of one object to incorporate the structure of another object, plus its own additions. This is a key element of every object-oriented program, and it allows the designers to create a conceptually integrated application. Inheritance is a major technique for representing knowledge; it is used in the AI knowledge representation schemes known as frames and semantic networks, which strongly influenced the development of object-oriented design [125, 256]. Thus, by using inheritance, designers represent their knowledge of an application in the design of a program. One object is said to be a specialization of another if the first contains all the attributes of the second, plus additional attributes of its own. One common refinement is to define classes of objects, which are templates for actual objects. Objects are then instances of some class, and inheritance is defined by specializations amongst classes rather than individual objects [211, 274].

Polymorphism is the idea of using a single name to represent logically similar operations, in much the same way that the '+' sign is used for both integer and floating-point multiplication in C. Polymorphic operations are mapped to the correct method by examining the signature of the operator call. Two logically similar methods might share the same name, but the exact parameters to be passed will *not* be the same. This allows the computer's run-time system to differentiate between calls to these two methods [211, 274].

An object-oriented design is usually a web of classes and sub-classes. In some languages, the inheritance relationships form a simple tree structure; a class may inherit the attributes of only one other class. In other languages, classes may inherit the attributes of more than one class. This is called multiple inheritance, and it seems to be out of vogue in the object-oriented design community. The C++ language supports multiple inheritance; the newer Java language does not [211, 274]. Objects in the program (which are the only entities that have storage allocated to them) communicate via message passing. A message is a call from one object to a method in a different object. These calls may be to polymorphic methods, or to non-polymorphic methods. In essence, an object-oriented program is ideally a group of objects that interact in order to accomplish some task [211].

## 1.2.3.4 Design Patterns

Design patterns are a formal mechanism for communicating software designs. They are prose text, not code, and thus cannot be used directly as building blocks of a system. They are applicable to any software system, rather than being restricted to a design paradigm such as OO design. There is, however, great excitement about the use and re-use of patterns for design problems, particularly within the OO community.

Patterns describe a problem, the context in which that problem occurs, a solution to that problem, and any tradeoffs involved in using that solution. A number of case studies have shown that using patterns facilitates communication between designers and encourages the re-use of proven solutions for a given problem [15, 241]. There have been workshops on design patterns at OOPSLA, a major conference on object-oriented technologies, since 1991, and a separate conference on design patterns (Pattern Languages of Programming) has been running since 1994 [15].

The heart of the design patterns movement is a standard template for describing a pattern. The different sections provide a standard structure that conveys all the information required to determine if a pattern is appropriate for use in a given problem. The template for a pattern is [32]:

*Name:* A descriptive name for the pattern
*Intent:* A rationale for, and description of the problem solved by, the pattern
*Also Known As:* Any other aliases for this pattern
*Motivation:* An illustrative example of how the pattern should be used
*Applicability:* The problem domain and situations in which the pattern should be used
*Structure:* A graphical representation of the class hierarchy in the pattern
*Participants:* What classes and objects are used in the pattern, and what their roles are
*Collaborations:* A description of how the participants interact to accomplish the goals of the pattern
*Consequences:* The tradeoffs that must be made and the expected results of using the pattern
*Implementation:* Any particular implementation details that a user should be aware of
*Sample Code:* Code fragments that provide hints on implementation issues
*Known Uses:* Real-world examples that use this pattern
*Related Patterns:* Cross-reference to related patterns, hints on which patterns should be used with this one

Patterns are not encapsulated solutions. A programmer using a pattern must map the classes and objects discussed in the pattern to the entities in their own program, which can be a difficult undertaking. Some automated tool support is described in [32] and [79], while links to a variety of pattern libraries may be found at [104], the homepage of the Hillside Group (an association of researchers interested in design patterns).

### 1.2.3.5 Maintenance Cycle

Most of a software system's lifetime will be spent in operation and undergoing maintenance. Software maintenance consists of changing the source code of a software system, usually for one of three reasons: system correction, system adaptation, and system perfection. System correction activities are undertaken when software errors are uncovered or failures occur, and consist of repairing the fault(s) responsible. One example is the patch released by Microsoft in August 2002 to correct a security flaw in Internet Explorer [194]. System adaptation activities are responses to changes in the operating environment of the software, which necessitate software changes. One might argue that fixing the Year 2000 bug was an adaptive, rather than corrective, maintenance task, as the software in question never included successful interpretation of $21^{st}$-century dates in its original specification. Finally, perfective maintenance is a catch-all term for the various changes to a software system required to meet the evolving needs of its users [232].

Software maintenance is basically a cyclic process, consisting of the eight stages shown in Figure 1.6. A *change cycle* begins with a change request, which is analyzed for required costs and resources and its expected impact. The change will be added to a list of changes to be implemented in the next release of the software system in the scheduling phase. The scheduled changes are implemented and tested, and then the existing user documentation is updated. There is a release or beta-testing phase before the changed system goes operational, and then the cycle begins again [232]. This is the point in the software's life cycle where the oft-stated assumption of software "immortality" breaks down. Software maintenance personnel are usually different from the original development team, and so do not have as deep an understanding of the software system. They will make errors, which over time will erode the software system's reliability. This is a peculiar form of aging; no physical decay occurs, just the slow breakdown of the system's conceptual integrity [87].

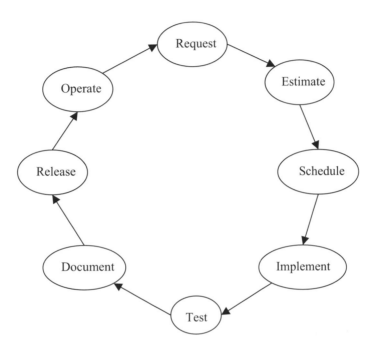

Figure 1.6: Maintenance Cycle [232]

### *1.2.4 New Directions*

The field of software engineering is a dynamic, fertile area of research and development. In this section, some of the more recent trends are summarized, including aspect-oriented programming, open-source development, and agile development methods.

Aspect-oriented programming is a recent innovation in programming language design. Object-oriented programs often contain routines that are used by several different object classes. In the old procedure-oriented languages, these routines would simply be child modules called by different parent modules. However, object-oriented languages do not make any provision for common routines between different classes of objects. Thus, in object-oriented languages, numerous copies of the same routine must be included as methods for different classes. If there is a later need to change these routines, the separate instances must be found and individually changed. *Aspects* are extensions to OO languages that centralize these multiple routines into one location. An aspect cuts across object boundaries, and thus represents a breaking of the modularity concepts that OO programming is based on; however, the proponents of aspect-oriented programming claim that aspects simply represent a different form of modularity.

Aspects are implemented by a language pre-processor. Points in an object where an aspect is required are tagged by the programmer, and the aspect is written separately. At compile time, the aspect will be inserted by the pre-processor, and then the entire program will be compiled as usual, along with the separate aspect code. There are several ongoing research projects in aspect-oriented programming, such as the AP/Demeter project at Northeastern University [164], the AspectJ language developed at Xerox PARC (now Palo Alto Research Center, Inc.) [224], and the MDSOC project at IBM [113].

Open-source development has become a significant force in the software engineering community. Open-source software is developed largely over the Internet. A core team of developers produces a product, and then places the source code into the public domain, protected by special licensing agreements. These agreements protect the ownership rights of the original code developers, but also permit others to download, read, modify and even redistribute the source code (provided the original copyright notices are not removed). The original source code, stored in a central repository, can only be modified with the approval of the core development team [221]. Thus, for instance, the Linux kernel (including all versions and patches) is archived at [137]. Anyone can download, modify and redistribute the source code. However, any changes to the official kernel have to be approved by Linus Torvalds and his team.

The open-source community is in large measure a backlash against commercial software vendors, who keep their source code proprietary. Open-source adherents claim two major advantages: first is that the code they produce is of superior quality, because more eyes are looking at each piece of code. The work products of the open-source community do seem to back up this claim; both the Linux operating system [137] and the Apache web server [5] enjoy good reputations for reliability. Apache, in fact, has a majority of the world-wide web server market [5], [201]. The second major claim of the open-source community is "freedom," that open-source development is in some way morally superior to proprietary development. This point of view is strongly espoused by the Open Source Initiative [221], the Free Software Foundation [83], and others. We attempt no analysis of this claim; issues of copyright ownership and freedom of information are far outside the scope of this study.

Agile development methods, including Extreme Programming (XP), are development techniques that put a premium on the development of code and minimize the organizational and project-management overhead. The ideas of agile development were summarized in February 2001 in the Manifesto for Agile Software Development [16]. The Manifesto declares that developers should emphasize:

- Individuals and interactions over processes and tools
- Working software over comprehensive documentation
- Customer collaboration over contract negotiation
- Responding to change over following a plan

Agile methods place a premium on iterative development procedures such as rapid prototyping, on close customer involvement, and on rapid response to changing requirements [105]. However, the most critical part of an agile development methodology is the quality of the programming team itself. Individual competency and talent are key factors for success in agile development projects [39]. This leads immediately to a fundamental criticism of agile methods: "There are only so many Kent Becks in the world to lead the team" [24]. Boehm views agile methods as part of a continuum of process models, ranging from completely ad-hoc arrangements to the tightest level of control, and indicates that agile methods are best suited to projects whose requirements undergo rapid change [24].

## 1.3 Artificial Intelligence in Software Engineering

If software engineering is fundamentally a learning process for the developers of a system, as argued in [29], then it only makes sense to use artificial intelligence to support human developers. Powerful AI tools for knowledge representation and reasoning are available, and can be useful for software development. Organizing and utilizing knowledge are critical tasks for any software project; as pointed out in [6], a software project typically involves the services of both *domain* experts and *software* experts. Domain experts possess extensive knowledge of the task a new software system will be asked to perform; in general, they will not have a detailed understanding of software development. Likewise, the software experts will have an extensive knowledge of how to design and implement software systems, but may have little to no experience in the application domain. The gap between these two pools of experience is a significant risk for any software system. Some authors (such as [42, 270]) have commented on an apparent hostility between the AI and software engineering communities; they ascribe this hostility to mutual misunderstanding and the fact that the two communities work on fundamentally similar problems. Given the essential role knowledge representation plays in both communities, this hostility is hopefully more appearance than reality.

There are currently three major thrusts in using artificial intelligence in software engineering: automatic programming, software reuse, and process modeling. Of these, automatic programming is far and away the oldest. In the 1960's, automatic programming meant the automatic generation of a machine readable program from a high-level description of that program. This goal was achieved with the development of automatic compilers. Automatic programming today means generating a machine-readable program from a high-level or natural language description of the problem to be solved [9, 204]. Software reuse is currently a significant research focus (especially for component-based software systems [14]), and process modeling encompasses a variety of tasks from cost estimation through creating a knowledge base to retain the developers' understanding of the software system.

Automatic programming is the "holy grail" for AI research in the software engineering domain. An automatic programming system, as envisioned by the AI community, would accept a set of specifications at a very high level of abstraction (even natural language), and would successively transform them into more detailed representations, arriving finally at compiled code. This would entirely remove humans from the business of coding large systems, an area in which human software engineers simply do not seem to be very effective. Maintenance would also be simplified; a change to the high-level system description would automatically be transformed into a new implementation of the system [9]. This goal remains elusive. A few automatic programming systems have been implemented; the REFINE tool, based on research at the Kestrel Institute [269], was a commercial automatic programming system marketed by Reasoning Systems, Inc., and the Programmer's Assistant project at MIT released their demonstration system KBEmacs more than 15 years ago [292]. However, neither system has been a commercial success. Other approaches include developing a system of correctness-preserving transforms to translate specifications into code [9, 75], using domain knowledge to interactively develop specifications [11], creating models to design and test formal requirements [31], and developing rule-based systems to help a programmer select the most appropriate UNIX utility [99]. There are also projects that try to develop automatic designers, based on experimental observations of human designers [1, 129, 273].

Reusability is a hot research topic in software engineering, because of the tremendous savings that could be realized if reusable components were widely available. A reusable component is a software artifact which can be removed from its original context, stored in a library, and inserted into a new program, thus saving the effort to develop that component from scratch. Not all software artifacts are reusable; in fact, reuse has to be designed into a component from the beginning [282]. The patterns community represents one attempt to promote reuse of design ideas; component libraries represent another. A component library is a collection of software components that have been designed and certified for reuse. In using a component library, the starting point is to develop a specification for a component that is to be inserted into a program. Next, a set of candidate components must be identified from the library, and each candidate must be evaluated for its suitability. Ultimately, one candidate is selected as being the best. Assuming that this candidate is reasonably close to the desired specification (otherwise the component will just be written from scratch), it will be modified as needed and then integrated into the program. Finally, the total experience of using this component will be recorded, and this information inserted into the component library's *experience base* for future reference [14]. The library's experience base contains a wealth of information in support of the software components in the library, and is vital to the successful use of the library (in fact, [14] considers the experience base to *be* the library, while source code is just one of many documents stored for each component). An experience based can be organized as a case-based reasoning system [281], as a more general analogical reasoning system [282], or as an expert system [2]. Some AI process models also incorporate software reuse [14, 219].

Software process models and support systems are used to organize a development project. The Capability Maturity Model discussed earlier requires that organizations develop an overall software engineering process, and then tailor that process to the particular needs of each project. However, the CMM does *not* provide a constructive mechanism for actually tailoring a process to a project. That is where process models come into play, and particularly AI process models. Process models support developers by rationalizing and improving communication, providing detailed reasoning about different features of the process, providing guidance to developers, automating certain process steps, and providing a mechanism for process improvement [49]. AI process models accomplish these tasks by using knowledge representation schemes as in [49], creating expert systems for software costing [60], or using the Goal-Question-Metric technique [14, 219].

There are a number of other proposals for using AI technology in software engineering, which do not conveniently fit into a specific category. One suggestion, found in [213], is to use communities of agents as the basic building block of software systems. Some of the benefits claimed include better fault tolerance and an explicit description of exception conditions. An automatic theorem prover is used in [131] to check for incomplete specifications, and to generate test cases for systems that have complete specifications. AI support for iterative development and rapid prototyping is described in [57] and [173]; the idea is that since AI systems are developed through exploratory programming, the tools for AI development would be very useful for generating system prototypes in a general software engineering project. There are also a number of computationally intelligent approaches for supporting software engineers. Computational Intelligence and computationally intelligent approaches to software engineering are reviewed in the next two sections.

## 1.4 Computational Intelligence

Computational Intelligence (CI) is a term coined in 1994 to describe several synergistic intelligent technologies that are effective in modeling systems, processes and decision making under uncertain conditions with incomplete and/or imprecise information [90]. According to Bezdek, "...a system is computationally intelligent when it: deals only with numerical (low-level) data, has a pattern recognition component, and does not use knowledge in the AI sense; and additionally when it (begins to) exhibit (i) computational adaptivity; (ii) computational fault tolerance; (iii) speed approaching human-like turnaround, and (iv) error rates that approach human performance..." [19]. One of the fundamental characteristics of CI technologies is that they are complementary to one another, in that they represent different but synergistic avenues of representing uncertain situations and systems. Fuzzy sets and fuzzy logic model the imprecision and vagueness that are a part of human thought; neural networks and genetic algorithms are inductive learning algorithms that mimic the natural processes of neuron operation and evolution, and chaotic systems and fractal sets model the irregularity that underlies the seemingly ordered and predictable physical world around us. One of the core philosophies of CI is to match a problem to the modeling technique best suited to solve it, instead of adopting a one-size-fits-all approach. Thus, fuzzy sets have seen extensive use in expert systems, while neural networks have been widely used as intelligent classifiers. A very good introduction to computational intelligence may be found in [116]. There are also close relationships between CI and other technologies such as case based reasoning, machine learning and data mining.

### 1.4.1 Fuzzy Sets and Fuzzy Logic

A fuzzy set is a set to which elements may *partly* belong. Unlike a set in the usual sense, fuzzy sets do not divide a universe of discourse into elements and non-elements. Instead, the boundaries of a fuzzy set are vague and imprecise. Mathematically, a fuzzy set is a set of 2-tuples $(x,\mu)$, with $x \in U$ a member of some universal set $U$, and $\mu \in [0,1]$ a membership grade. The membership grade represents the degree to which elements belong to the fuzzy set; a grade of 0 means no membership, while a grade of 1 means total membership. The fuzzy set may also be considered a membership function $U \rightarrow [0,1]$ (analogous to a characteristic function for a set) [146].

Fuzzy sets capture that form of uncertainty called *vagueness* or *imprecision*. This form of uncertainty represents situations where a value is approximately known; it is distinct from the form of uncertainty known as randomness, because approximate quantities do not obey the law of large numbers [249]. In other words, repeated sampling of an approximate quantity does not cause the sample mean to converge to the theoretical population mean in the limit of infinite samples. This kind of uncertainty is a major feature of human language, and so fuzzy sets have been used to provide mathematical precision to phrases in natural language. This is done using linguistic variables, which are an association between a word in natural language and a fuzzy set. Linguistic variables were introduced in [305], and have found widespread application in the domain of automatic controllers, as first outlined in [177, 280]. These *fuzzy controllers* are similar to expert systems, in that their core functionality is a set of inference rules (the *rulebase*), which are fired in accordance with the rules of fuzzy logic [146]. Since any number of arbitrary rules may in theory be introduced into a fuzzy rulebase, fuzzy controllers provide a simple, intuitive way to construct strongly nonlinear controllers. Fuzzy systems have been shown to be universal approximators [291], and have even been applied to the control and modeling of chaotic systems [35, 287].

*Fuzzy numbers* are closely related to linguistic variables. A fuzzy number is a fuzzy set that represents a number that is not precisely known. Fuzzy numbers are defined on the set of real numbers; one particular real number $x$ has a maximum membership value, and the membership value of any other real number $y$ monotonically decreases as the distance between $x$ and $y$ increases. Intuitively, this means that the membership of $x$ in the fuzzy number $F$ should be 1, while the membership function of $F$ is unimodal. Formally, a fuzzy number is a convex, normal fuzzy subset $F$ of the real line with membership function $\mu$, where normality means that $\max(\mu(x)) = 1$ and convexity means that

$$\mu(\lambda x_1 + (1 - \lambda)x_2) \geq \min(\mu(x_1), \mu(x_2)) \tag{1.1}$$

for all $x, x_1, x_2 \in R, \lambda \in [0,1]$. An example of a fuzzy number is depicted in Figure 1.7. The definition of convexity ensures that $\mu$ is unimodal, with its peak at $x$, conforming to our intuition [146].

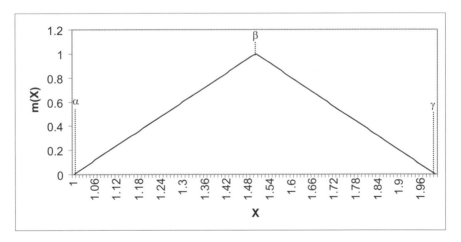

Figure 1.7: Fuzzy Number

Recently, the idea of granular computing has been a major research focus of the fuzzy systems community. Granular computing involves reasoning about groups of objects rather than individual objects. Briefly, objects in a universe of discourse are aggregated into groups (or *granules*), and then computations are carried out using the granules as atomic objects [306]. This notion is also called "Computing with Words" [307], since a word can be considered the label of a fuzzy set. The main issues in granular computing are first, how is this aggregation performed, and second, how are these granules used once they are formed? Zadeh provided some suggestions on those points in [308]; other views may be found in [25, 54, 163, 187, 229].

### *1.4.2 Artificial Neural Networks*

Artificial Neural Networks (ANNs) are inductive learning algorithms that mimic the operation of neurons in animal brains. An ANN is a directed graph in which each vertex is a computational node, and each edge is a link to another node (see Figure 1.8). ANNs derive their power from having a large number of simple computational units that are very densely interconnected [101]. The earliest paper on ANNs was [182] in 1943; other important early papers included [102] and [212]. Rosenblatt's single-layer Perceptron architecture [252] was very popular in the 1960's, until Minsky and Papert showed that it could not solve any learning problem that was not linearly separable [199]. The comment at the end of this proof, casting doubt that a multi-layer perceptron would fare any better, resulted in a 15-year chill on the development of ANNs. However, in 1983, Rumelhart demonstrated a learning algorithm, based on backward-propagation in a multilayer perceptron, which *could* solve problems that were not linearly separable [255]. (The same algorithm was found to have been independently discovered by Werbos in 1974 [294].) A few years later, multiplayer perceptrons using Rumelhart's Backpropagation architecture were shown to be universal approximators [44], and they are now accepted as powerful and flexible inductive learning algorithms. Since that time, a staggering number of papers on ANNs have been published; see the journal *IEEE Transactions on Neural Networks* for further reading.

In common with other inductive learning algorithms, ANNs learn by repeatedly observing a set of input-output pairings, and developing an internal representation of the underlying function. The internal representation used by ANNs is a pattern of connection weights. Each link between two nodes in an ANN has an associated weight, which is altered by the learning algorithm of the ANN. Thus, ANNs employ a distributed form of knowledge, rather than centralizing it in a rulebase. ANNs are particularly well-suited to the control of highly nonlinear plants, whose dynamics are not fully understood but which can be effectively controller by an experienced operator. The ANN is exposed to repeated observations consisting of plant state variables and operator responses, and is trained to find a relationship between the two [101].

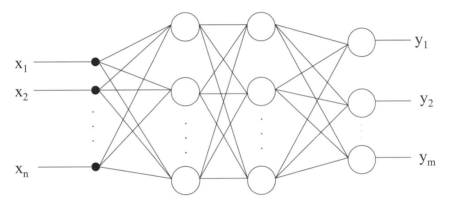

Figure 1.8: Neural Network

The Backpropagation learning algorithm Rumelhart et al. developed for multilayer perceptrons is a form of gradient descent. As such, it is vulnerable to local minima in weight space. A number of techniques for forcing Backpropagation networks out of a local minimum have been proposed in the literature. One of the simplest is adding a momentum term to the Backpropagation formula, which adds an additional vector to the current weight update [101]. Other schemes include the hybrid neuro-fuzzy systems we discuss later, Newton's method, or conjugate gradient algorithms[116].

### *1.4.3 Genetic Algorithms*

Genetic algorithms are optimization schemes, much like neural networks. However, genetic algorithms do not appear to suffer from local minima as badly as neural networks do. Genetic algorithms are based on the model of evolution, in which a population evolves towards overall fitness, even though individuals perish. Evolution dictates that superior individuals have a better chance of reproducing than inferior individuals, and thus are more likely to pass their superior traits on to the next generation. This "survival of the fittest" criterion was first converted to an optimization algorithm by Holland in 1975 [108], and is today a major optimization technique for complex, nonlinear problems [193].

In a genetic algorithm, each individual of a population is one possible solution to an optimization problem, encoded as a binary string called a chromosome. A group of these individuals will be generated, and will compete for the right to reproduce or even be carried over into the next generation of the population. Competition consists of applying a fitness function to every individual in the population; the individuals with the best result are the fittest. The next generation will then be constructed by carrying over a few of the best individuals, reproduction, and mutation. Reproduction is carried out by a "crossover" operation, similar to what happens in an animal embryo. Two chromosomes exchange portions of their code, thus forming a pair of new individuals. In the simplest form of crossover, a crossover point on the two chromosomes is selected at random, and the chromosomes exchange all data after that point, while keeping their own data up to that point. In order to introduce additional variation in the population, a mutation operator will randomly change a bit or bits in some chromosome(s). Usually, the mutation rate is kept low to permit good solutions to remain stable [193].

The two most critical elements of a genetic algorithm are the way solutions are represented, and the fitness function, both of which are problem-dependent. The coding for a solution must be designed to represent a possibly complicated idea or sequence of steps. The fitness function must not only interpret the encoding of solutions, but also must establish a ranking of different solutions. The fitness function is what will drive the entire population of solutions towards a globally best solution. Usually, developing the fitness function is the most difficult part of preparing a genetic algorithm, and currently there is no constructive method for ensuring the population will in fact converge to a global optimum [193]. For further reading, we suggest the updated version of Holland's book, [109].

### 1.4.4 Fractal Sets and Chaotic Systems

The notion of fractal sets begins with a fairly simple mathematical question: what is a continuous function? The conventional answer is that a continuous function is one that is differentiable everywhere, or at worst has finitely many points at which no derivative exists. Intuitively, a continuous function should be smooth in appearance. However, if one points to any physical object, this idea of continuity breaks down. Under microscopic examination, even a surface that appears smooth to the naked eye will show considerable irregularities. In fact, this phenomenon persists as we examine the object at finer and finer length scales. No length scale is ever reached where the surface becomes a smooth curve. How to account for this phenomenon [178]?

A classic example is the question, "How long is the coast of Great Britain?" The answer is, it depends on the scale of the observations. Measuring the coast on a scale of kilometers will give a far different answer than measuring it on a scale of inches. Fine irregularities appear at shorter and shorter length scales, making it impossible to reach a single answer for the question [178, 286]. In general, a fractal curve will be a continuous, nowhere-differentiable curve, having unique geometric properties [303]. Likewise, a fractal set is an arbitrary set which has a power-law relationship between the size (in some sense) of its constituent elements and their frequency. For example, given a collection of objects, the number $N$ of these objects with a linear dimension greater than r should obey the relation

$$N = \frac{C}{r^D} \tag{1.2}$$

where $C$ is a constant, and the power $D$ is the dimension of the set. If $D$ is a non-integer value, then the set is a fractal [286].

More formally, consider the dimension of an arbitrary set. Define the dimension operator as follows:

## Definition 1.1 [303]

Given some set $X \subset \mathbf{R}^n$, the dimension of $X$, denoted by $\dim(X)$, must satisfy four properties:

1.     a) For a one-element set $X = \{p\}$, $\dim(X) = 0$.
       b) For the unit interval $X = I^1$, $\dim(X) = 1$
       c) For the unit hypercube $X = I^m$, $\dim(X) = m$.
2. (Monotonicity) If $X \subset Y$, then $\dim(X) \leq \dim(Y)$
3. Given a sequence of sets $X_j \subset \mathbf{R}^n$,

$$\dim\left(\bigcup_{j=1}^{\infty} X_j\right) = \sup_j \dim(X_j) \tag{1.3}$$

4. (Invariance) Given a homeomorphism $\varphi$ from $\mathbf{R}^n$ to $\mathbf{R}^n$, $\dim(\varphi(X)) = \dim(X)$.

Ordinary points, lines, geometric shapes and geometric solids clearly have a dimension that obeys these four conditions. For more general sets, the topological dimension $\dim_T$ is a mathematically sound way to define a dimension. The topological dimension generalizes the fact that a ball is a three-dimensional object, but the surface of a sphere is a two-dimensional object; the dimension of an arbitrary set is inferred via induction from the dimension of its boundary. There is another way to define dimensions for arbitrary sets, known as the Hausdorff dimension $\dim_H$. For most ordinary sets, the topological and Hausdorff dimensions are identical. However, where the topological dimension can take on only integer values, the Hausdorff dimension is real-valued, and is known to always be greater than or equal to the topological dimension. The basic definition of a fractal set $X$ in $\mathbf{R}^n$ is that the topological and Hausdorff dimensions for $X$ are different, namely

$$\dim_T(X) < \dim_H(X) \Rightarrow X \text{ is a fractal set} \tag{1.4}$$

In particular, if the Hausdorff dimension is not an integer, then $X$ is necessarily a fractal set [303].

One famous example of a fractal set is the Cantor set. This set is generated by a recursive procedure, as follows: partition the unit interval into three equal subintervals, and delete the middle interval. Then apply the same procedure to each of the remaining sub-intervals. After an infinite number of repetitions, a completely disconnected set of points is obtained, whose topological dimension is 0 (see Figure 1.9). However, the Hausdorff dimension of the Cantor set is log 2/log 3 ≈ 0.63092, and thus the Cantor set is a fractal set. In general, such simple proofs that a set has a fractal geometry are very difficult to construct. The problem is that accurately computing a Hausdorff dimension, or bounding it from below, are very difficult problems. Bounding the Hausdorff dimension from above is considerably easier, but this does not show that a set is a fractal [303].

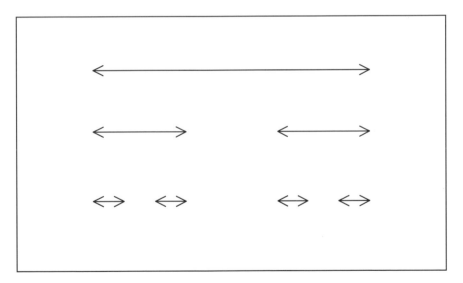

Figure 1.9: Two Iterations of the Cantor Set [303]

There *is* a class of fractal sets for which the Hausdorff dimension is easily calculated. These are the famous *self-similar* sets, which include the Cantor set. The basic definition of self-similarity is based on the notion of a contraction. A contraction is some mapping $\varphi \colon \mathbf{R}^n \to \mathbf{R}^n$ such that

$$\|\varphi(x) - \varphi(y)\| \le c\|x - y\| \qquad (1.5)$$

for some $c \in (0,1)$ and any $x,y \in \mathbf{R}^n$. The definition of self-similarity is as follows.

## Definition 1.2 [303]

A non-empty compact set $X \subset \mathbf{R}^n$ is self-similar if, for some set of contractions $\{\varphi_1, \varphi_2, ..., \varphi_m\}$ ($m \ge 2$), the following relation holds:

$$X = \bigcup_{i=1}^{m} \varphi i(X) \qquad (1.6)$$

If the maps $\varphi_j$ also happen to be linear, then the set is called a self-affine set. Any self-affine set is self-similar, and any self-similar set is a fractal set, as depicted in Figure 1.10 [303].

There is a very close relationship between fractal sets and chaotic systems. A chaotic system is an analytic function that cannot be accurately determined from observation of its behavior over any time span. What this means is that any prediction of future behavior based on past behavior is inaccurate; the amplitude of the prediction error very quickly becomes as large as the original signal. This is the signature property of a chaotic system; any two trajectories that are infinitesimally close at some point in the system state space will diverge from each other at an exponential rate. Thus, even the slightest prediction error is magnified exponentially through time. The relationship between fractals and chaos is simply that fractal sets can be the generators of a chaotic system, and the invariant set or attractor of a chaotic system will have a fractal geometry [130, 303].

The literature on using chaos theory to analyze time series data has become quite extensive. At this time, Kantz and Schreiber's monograph [130] is generally considered to be the best resource on the subject. As discussed in detail in Chapter 3, chaotic time series analysis involves a number of steps and requires considerable judgment on the part of the analyst. Chaos theory and fractal sets fit into the soft computing paradigm because they can usefully model a type of uncertainty called *irregularity*, which deals with rare events, intermittency, bifurcations, and other such behaviors. They are a better fit for these phenomena than the techniques of probability theory, which models the form of uncertainty called *randomness*, or fuzzy sets which model *vagueness* and *imprecision*.

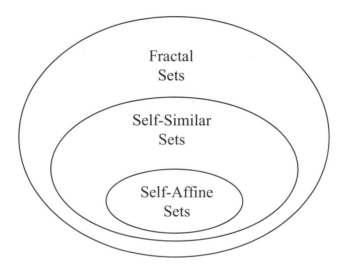

Figure 1.10: Hierarchy of Fractal Sets [303]

### *1.4.5 Combined CI Methods*

One of the distinguishing characteristics of computationally intelligent techniques is that they are complementary to one another, and the various hybridizations of these techniques can be more effective than any one of them in isolation. The best known of these hybrids are the neuro-fuzzy systems, which are hybrids of fuzzy logic and neural networks. In these hybrids, the interpretative power of fuzzy systems and the learning power of a neural network are combined. This overcomes the main deficiencies of both technologies, to wit that a fuzzy system is not designed to learn, and the distributed knowledge in neural networks is very difficult to interpret. Indeed, pure fuzzy systems and pure neural networks are now seen as the extreme points of a continuum of intelligent systems, in which a tradeoff must be made between clarity and adaptability [116].

The first papers on neuro-fuzzy systems were written by Lee and Lee in 1974 [158, 159]. Lee and Lee generalized the McCullogh-Pitts neuron, permitting inputs and outputs in the closed interval [0,1] instead of the set {0,1}. Kandel and Lee published the first book that included a discussion of fuzzy neural networks in 1979 [127]. Keller and Hunt generalized the Perceptron algorithm to produce a fuzzy hyperplane as the decision boundary, instead of a crisp hyperplane in [136]. The entire field of neuro-fuzzy systems received a major boost at the 1$^{st}$ NASA Workshop on Neural Networks and Fuzzy Logic in 1988 [279]. This was a watershed event, and a tremendous number of papers on neuro-fuzzy architecture have been published in the intervening years. Probably the best-known of these are Jang's ANFIS architecture [115] and Pal and Mitra's fuzzy MLP [222, 223].

A number of other hybrid systems have also been proposed in the literature on computational intelligence. For instance, genetic algorithms can be used to provide a learning capability for fuzzy systems, yielding a fuzzy-genetic hybrid such as in [246]. An even more ambitious hybrid is the FuGeNeSys architecture in [257], where each individual in a genetic algorithm represents a neuro-fuzzy system. An individual is inserted by instantiating that neuro-fuzzy system, training it, and returning it to the population. There are also hybrids of chaotic systems and neural networks [144], and fuzzy systems, neural networks, and wavelet transforms (which are related to chaotic systems and fractal sets) in [106].

### *1.4.6 Case Based Reasoning*

Case-Based Reasoning (CBR) is a way to solve new problems by examining solutions to similar problems that have been encountered in the past. A CBR system stores information about known problems and their solutions in an experience base. When a new problem is encountered, the system searches for similar problems in the experience base. The solutions to those similar problems are then modified, in order to account for the differences between those old problems and the new one. These two elements – judging similarity between problems instead of equivalence, and reasoning about what the solution to a new, unseen problem should be – are what differentiate CBR systems from a database query. Solutions are not merely retrieved by an equivalence relation, they are found by a more general *similarity* relation (which can be viewed as a fuzzy form of equivalence) and adapted to fit the new problem [53].

Each stored problem, together with its solution, is a case in the CBR experience base. Cases are stored by recording all relevant attributes of a problem and a description of the solution. When a new problem is encountered, the attributes of that problem are extracted, and sent to the experience base as a *probe*. Similarity between a probe and a case is determined by a distance measure, which has to be defined for the specific problem. For purely numeric attributes, a Euclidean distance is one possibility; for a mix of numeric and nominal attributes, a mix of numeric and symbolic distance measures might need to be used. Other possibilities include using a neural network or statistical models to calculate a distance. As a rule, distance is inversely proportional to similarity, so the cases with the minimum distance to the probe are the most similar. CBR systems are most useful in situations where an approximate solution is acceptable; there is only low to moderate interaction between attributes; and there are discontinuities in the relations between attributes. The latter would be the case when, for instance, there is a linear relationship between two real-valued variables, but only within a specific interval for each variable. The main overheads for CBR systems are in computing the similarity between stored cases and the probe, and determining how to modify existing solutions. Depending on the problem domain, the modification subsystem might be a full expert system in its own right [53]. The use of similarity for finding candidate cases, and approximate reasoning to generate solutions to new problems, tie CBR closely to CI technologies. Both are geared towards decision-making in uncertain environments, and both exploit the notion of approximate solutions.

### 1.4.7 Machine Learning

The discipline of machine learning involves efforts to make computers imitate human cognition. Machine learning researcher hope to create artificial systems that can learn the way human beings do, and can thus tackle the difficult problems we humans are very good at, such as recognizing a friendly face. They also hope to discover more about how we ourselves learn new concepts by building artificial learners [210, 256]. There are two ways that machine learning researchers could attack this problem. The first is to create a computer simulation of the human brain and expose the simulation to a wealth of experience, in the same way that humans are exposed to new experiences from birth. Such a simulation is plainly out of reach. The second avenue of attack is to create algorithms that will simulate a class of input-output behaviors, and thus mimic the *observable* behavior of human cognition. The inductive learning schemes that are generally referred to as "machine learning algorithms," such as neural networks, genetic algorithms and clustering, are all examples of this sort of algorithm. The machine learning community concentrates on this second line of attack.

Plainly, some of the core technologies in CI are also machine learning algorithms, and so there is considerable overlap between the two areas. However, this overlap is more than merely common algorithms; machine learning and CI fundamentally deal with reasoning under conditions of uncertainty, and so share both philosophical and practical concerns. The basic philosophical problem both communities wrestle with is the problem of induction: how to create models based on samples of past experience that remain valid when encountering new inputs or situations, and what are the limits of these models. Chaotic systems represent the most extreme limits on machine learning, as they do not remain predictable for more than a very short time horizon. At a more mundane level, there is a need to evaluate both how accurate a model is, and to understand when that model could be invalidated by events in the real world. This is a very important consideration for data mining, the most widely-deployed application of machine learning in industry. Data mining is thus embedded in the Knowledge Discovery in Databases (KDD) framework, also referred to as *business intelligence.*

### 1.4.8 Data Mining

Knowledge Discovery in Databases (KDD) is the process of distilling useful information from a large collection of data. Data tables with numerous attributes and a large number of records are extremely difficult for humans to understand, and databases with multiple large tables are even worse. Therefore, various types of summarizations of a database are needed in order for human beings to make use of the information in that database. KDD is a framework for obtaining such summarizations. KDD and data mining are sometimes used interchangeably; however, a more relevant usage for our purposes comes from Fayyad [74], in which "data mining" is one step in the KDD framework. Fayyad defines KDD as a sequence of nine steps:

i.   Defining the goal of the KDD process
ii.  Assembling a dataset from a data warehouse, and perhaps selecting a subset of the data for analysis
iii. Data cleaning & preprocessing
iv.  Feature reduction
v.   Selecting the data mining task (prediction, classification, etc.)
vi.  Selecting the data mining algorithm (neural networks, regression analysis, clustering, etc.)
vii. Data mining
viii. Evaluation of the data mining results
ix.  Consolidating the results with prior knowledge, and applying them.

Data mining is a search for associations in a database that may be corrupted with noise, contain missing values, and may be absolutely gigantic in size. These characteristics make CI algorithms excellent candidates for data mining algorithms. Other possible data mining tools include statistical regression and correlation algorithms, or rule extraction schemes [74, 155, 156, 157], among many others.

## 1.5 Computational Intelligence in Software Engineering

Computationally intelligent technologies find a somewhat different use in software engineering than traditional AI techniques. Where AI systems concentrate on knowledge representation and automatic programming, computationally intelligent systems focus on system modeling and decision making in the presence of uncertainty. This does not mean that the two do not converge on some common areas of interest within software engineering; there is in fact a rich literature on using computational intelligence for estimating software project costs [22, 77, 233, 272]. A survey of this material may be found in [94].

Other applications of computational intelligence to software engineering focus on a variety of sources and forms of uncertainty in software development. As argued in [96], computationally intelligent systems can play an important role because there are multiple levels of uncertainty in a software system, and possibly multiple *degrees* of uncertainty. Neural networks are used to assign routines and objects to software modules in [263]; they key idea in that paper is to treat modularization as a problem of categorization. Linguistic variables are used in formal specifications in [124]. The linkage of linguistic terms with a specified fuzzy set discussed in Section 1.4.1 makes these specifications intuitively understandable, and yet still mathematically precise. Finally, decision trees are used to filter reusable components from a given software system in [248]. There is also an extensive list of publications on analyzing software metrics using computationally intelligent systems; we defer our review of this material until Chapter 4.

## 1.6 Remarks

Software engineering is a huge and complicated undertaking, and the resulting products are the most complex technological systems in the world today. An overview of software engineering, and of the AI and computationally intelligent technologies that are now being examined as possible aids in the software engineering process, was the focus of this chapter. In the next chapter, a more detailed review of the process of testing a piece of software – usually the single largest expense in a project – will be undertaken. Brooks estimated that an ordinary software development project should expect 50% of its resources to be expended on testing; in the case of safety-critical systems, that figure could rise to 80% [29].

# Chapter 2

# Software Testing and Artificial Intelligence

## 2.1 Introduction

The focus of this chapter is on the quality of software, and how software testing is an essential component of a software quality plan. Testing has been a part of software development from the very beginning; Alan Turing himself wrote an article entitled "Checking out a large routine" as part of a 1950 manual [196]. It is a major part of every software development project; Brooks has stated that 50% of the development resources in an ordinary project (and up to 80% of resources in a safety-critical system) will be spent in testing. To begin this review, "software quality" will be defined, and then various testing methodologies will be described. Finally, AI and computationally intelligent techniques for software testing are reviewed.

## 2.2 Software Quality

"Quality" is one of those engineering terms that are intuitively simple but difficult to define exactly. At the most basic level, quality means how well some product performs in use. This is a customer's perception, and does not directly translate into engineering specifications. A more technical meaning is that quality is the "degree of excellence" of a product, considering all relevant characteristics of the product. Thus, issues such as reliability, performance and usability contribute to a system's overall quality in that they are some of the quality characteristics of this product. High quality will then mean a high degree of excellence in these and other characteristics [92]. Quality is thus an evaluation of a product in its totality.

Software quality is perhaps the most critical technological challenge of the 21$^{st}$ century. No other product in the industrialized world is so labor-intensive, and none are as error-prone [121, 122]. Several software characteristics have become legendary for their poor quality. Reliability, of course, is at the very top of this list; software "bugs" are by definition failures. Usability has also been cited as a concern in innumerable software projects. Thus, "improving software quality" is a mammoth undertaking for any organization, requiring improvements in a number of areas. One technique for improving the quality of a software system (and its accompanying non-code work products) is the use of formal inspections at the requirements, design and coding stages. Jones [122] reports an average improvement of 15% in software productivity when inspections are used.

Despite the usefulness of inspections, software testing necessarily remains the basic mechanism for assessing software quality. Since large software systems can have $10^{20}$ states or more [84], software testing is and most likely will always be non-exhaustive. In other words, software test cases are samples of the complete input space of a program. There is, however, no substitute for actually testing a program; we cannot determine if a program is correct or not by merely inspecting the source code. To be specific, consider a general-purpose computer language, capable of simulating a Turing machine. Given an arbitrary program in this language, and an arbitrary input, no algorithm can be designed that will determine if an arbitrary statement in the program will execute or not. Furthermore, while programs exist for which this analysis is possible, no algorithm can be fashioned that will distinguish programs for which this analysis is possible from those for which it is *not* possible. If this last statement were not true, then the halting problem for Turing machines would be solvable [72].

Quality management is an ongoing comparison of the actual quality of a product with its expected quality. In the field of software development, software metrics are collected at various points in the development cycle, and utilized to guide testing and quality improvement efforts [47, 68]. Metrics are used to identify modules in software systems that are potentially error-prone, so that extra development, testing and maintenance effort can be directed at those modules. One of the empirical facts known about software failures is that they tend to cluster in a few modules. An oft-quoted rule is that 80% of a system's bugs will be found in just 20% of the system's modules [30, 141]. Metrics are also used by program managers to track the current status of a project; these metrics tend to be related to cost and schedule, rather than source code. While these metrics are vital elements of both traditional and component-based system development, [30, 265], they are outside the scope of this study.

A wide variety of regression models for relating software metrics to defect rates have been investigated, including robust regression, local polynomial regression, Poisson regression, and M-estimation [93]. However, there is currently no theoretical model relating metric values to defect rates, and so selecting a regression model is a trial-and-error process. This means that we are searching an infinite space of model *forms*, selecting one of them and then fitting that model to our software quality data. The use of machine learning algorithms is partly motivated by that fact that non-parametric models such as neural networks or genetic algorithm need far less detailed *a priori* information to construct a model for a given dataset.

Each software metric quantifies some characteristic of a program. Simple counting metrics such as the number of lines of source code or Halstead's number of operators and operands [97, 118] simply describe how many "things" there are in a program. More complex metrics such as McCabe's cyclomatic complexity [181] or the Bandwidth metric [232] attempt to describe the "complexity" of a program, by measuring the number of decisions in a module or the average level of nesting in the module, respectively. While different metrics do measure different characteristics, the various metrics tend to be strongly correlated to each other and to the number of failures in a program [67, 167]. Furthermore, there tend to be relatively few modules in any given system that will have a high degree of complexity. As a result, any database of software characteristics or failures will be heavily skewed towards simple modules with a low occurrence of failures [8].

```
worker(int buf[], int low, int high, int step){
int min, max;
int i;

1   min = buf[low];
2   max = buf[low];
3   i = low + step;
4   while (i < high){
5       if (max < buf[i]){
6               max = buf[i];
        }
7       if (min > buf[i]){
8               min = buf[i];
        }
9       i = i + step
        }
10 printf ("%d\n",min);
11 printf ("%d\n",max);
}
```

Figure 2.1: Worker Function (Translated from [147])

Two important tools used in developing software metrics are the *control graph* and the *call graph*. The control graph is a directed graph representing the flow of control in a program. Each vertex in the graph represents a statement, and each edge in the graph represents a direct transfer of control from one statement to the next. Two sequential statements will be linked by an edge; a branch statement will be linked to the first statements in each of the possible paths from that branch. Loops are represented as cycles, and thus each possible element of the structured programming paradigm maps directly to a graphical construct [48]. As an example, consider the C program in Figure 2.1, translated from Pascal in [147]. This program has two conditional statements, nested within one loop construct. The control graph for this program may be found in Figure 2.2; based on this control graph, the cyclomatic complexity of this module is 4 [181, 275].

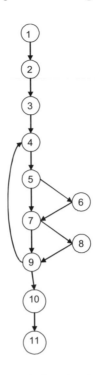

Figure 2.2: Control Flow Graph for Figure 2.1

The call graph of a program is a directed graph that represents how modules in the program call each other. Each subroutine (function, procedure, method, etc.) is represented as a vertex in the graph, and an edge from vertex $P_i$ to vertex $P_j$ means that $P_i$ directly calls $P_j$. A recursive call to a subroutine is represented by a cycle in the graph; purely recursive routines call themselves, while a cycle of two or more vertexes denotes indirect recursion. The fan-in and fan-out metrics are based on analyzing call graphs, and are widely used in industry [126]. As an example, the subroutines in Figure 2.3 lead to the call graph in Figure 2.4 [183, 258]. These figures also point out some of the aspects of program behavior that are *not* represented in the call graph. As the reader will note, the output of the program in Figure 2.3 is "Hello World". However, this fact cannot be deduced from an inspection of the call graph, because timing information is not contained in the call graph.

```
int main(){
      sub1();
      return 0;
}
void sub1(){
      sub2();
      sub3();
}
void sub2(){
      sub4();
}
void sub3(){
      sub5();
}
void sub4(){
      printf("Hello ");
}
void sub5(){
      printf("World\n");
}
```

Figure 2.3: Hello World in C

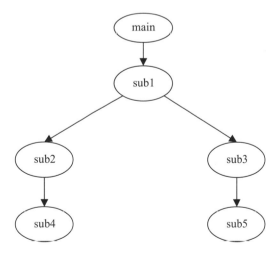

Figure 2.4: Call Graph for Figure 2.3

## 2.3 Software Testing

Software testing is an effort to find system inputs that will trigger the failure of a software system. Finding these inputs can be extremely difficult, particularly in the late stages of testing. The conditions that will trigger a latent fault can be extremely complex, and in fact one fault can "hide" behind another one [84]. Testing activities will normally consume 50% of a software project's resources, and can consume up to 80% of the resources in a safety-critical project [29]. Unfortunately, debugging remains a labor-intensive, manual process; in fact, a 1997 article reported that many programmers still prefer the manual insertion of "print" statements as their debugging technique of choice [165]. An informal 1997 survey reported in [69] indicated that manual techniques, such as inserting print statements, manually executing a test case, or inserting breakpoints, accounted for 78% of real-world programmers' attempts to solve exceptionally difficult bugs.

In the remainder of this book, we adopt the failure model advocated by Voas [84], Laprie and Kanoun [152], and others. In this model, a *fault* is a mistake in the source code of a program. As such, it is a static entity. A fault may be exercised by some input to the software; that is, the input causes the flow of control in the program to pass through the location of a fault. If that exercised fault causes an internal departure of the program state from its correct value, then an *error* has occurred. If that error manages to propagate all the way to the system output, then it becomes a *failure*. Failures are the observed departure of a program from its correct behavior. Note that not all faults will trigger an error, and not all errors will result in failures. Faults that do not result in failures when they are exercised are said to be "hiding." This model accounts for much of the complicated behavior of software failures, by explaining how errors may mask one another, or how faults can remain undetected for years only to manifest themselves in unusual situations or a changed environment.

Whittaker and Jorgensen [296] have developed a classification scheme for software faults, dividing them into four broad classes: improperly constrained inputs, improperly constrained stored data, improperly constrained computation, and improperly constrained outputs. An improperly constrained input is an input that violates the assumptions of the software; an example in [296] is a shellsort program in which an array of data and the length of the array are parameters to the shellsort function. Neither the array length, nor the existence of the array, is verified in the function; thus the program is trivially easy to break. Checking input constraints is a basic part of good programming practice as taught in computer science classes; however, Whittaker and Jorgensen found that this simple precaution is largely ignored. Improperly constraining stored data leads to a corruption of the program state, and thus to a failure. Improperly constrained computation refers to situations where the result of a computation on legal values is an illegal value (such as the one that destroyed Ariane-501). Arithmetic overflows and underflows are prominent examples of this kind of fault. Finally, failing to constrain an output is also a fault, since the user only perceives the output of a program [296].

When a failure is detected, software developers will attempt to debug the program. Ideally, the fault that caused the error will be identified and corrected, and no other part of the system will be adversely affected. In reality, the fault could have been incorrectly identified; alternatively, the repair could only partly remove the fault or might even introduce new faults. Finally, it is possible for one fault to hide behind another. This occurs when the error propagating from the hidden fault is overwritten by the error from the second fault. Thus, the perfect removal of one fault could expose a second, possibly more serious fault. Thus, the successful removal of a fault could actually make the software system *less* reliable than it was before [84]. An essential part of removing a fault is regression testing, in which a subset of the test suite is re-run to determine if the test cases that were correctly executed before the repair still execute correctly afterwards.

### 2.3.1 White-Box Testing

White-box testing (also known as glass-box or clear-box testing) is a testing methodology that explicitly makes use of the structure of a program. The goal is to increase the chances of finding errors in software by effectively increasing the density of errors. White-box testing schemes concentrate on program structures that are likely to be problematic, and ensure that the entire program is tested [66, 232]. Some white-box approaches include dataflow testing, partition testing, symbolic execution, state-based testing, program slicing, and mutation testing. Testing object-oriented programs will also introduce additional complexities

One of the main questions in white box testing is deciding how much testing is required. This question is addressed by code coverage criteria, which define the minimum standard of testing. For instance, statement testing simply requires that every statement in the program be executed by at least one test case. This criterion is considered very weak. A stronger criterion comes from branch testing, which demands that every logical branch in the program be executed at least once. The strongest criterion is path testing, which requires that every possible control path through the program be executed at least once. This criterion is generally considered infeasible, because the number of possible paths in a program with loop structures can be infinite [65]. There is also a family of coverage criteria called condition coverage, which are frequently used in the aerospace industry. For instance, *condition/decision* coverage stipulates that, in the course of testing, every entry and exit point in the program must be invoked, every condition in any decision statement must have taken on every possible value in its own domain, and every decision statement must have taken on all possible outcomes. A stronger version, *multiple-condition* coverage, requires that all entry and exit points are invoked, and every possible combination of conditional values in every decision statement is tested [37]. One of the weaknesses of using coverage criteria is that the criteria make no distinction between paths that a program can possibly traverse, and those that are impossible. In fact, the general problem of distinguishing between feasible and infeasible paths is undecidable [72, 215]; however, the simpler problem of constructing a path through a specified set of statements can be solved in $O(|E|)$ time, where $E$ is the number of edges in the program control graph [85]. Many papers comparing the different test criteria have been published; [82] is a good example, and refers to a number of other comparisons in the literature.

A specialized set of coverage criteria, known as data-flow criteria, has attracted a great deal of interest in recent years. Data-flow testing is a white-box testing strategy that grows out of dataflow analysis in optimizing compilers, in contrast to the control-flow methods discussed earlier. Essentially, dataflow testing concentrates on two particular uses of variables in a program: the points where a value is stored to a variable (a *definition*), and the points where the stored value of a variable is accessed (a *use*). The development of the dataflow approach is usually credited to Rapps and Weyuker in [247]; Laski and Korel published a similar approach at roughly the same time [154]. Efforts to ensure that the various dataflow criteria of [247] result in feasible test cases are reported in [81], while extensions to the dataflow criteria are described in [214].

Partition testing is an attempt to reduce the number of test cases in a program by finding homogenous regions within the input space. The idea is to find regions where a single test case can represent the entire input region it belongs to [250]. There are any number of criteria that can be used to partition the input space of a program; one suggestion from [288] is to cluster modules based on the number of accesses to shared variables. However, partition testing is very sensitive to how the partitions are determined; a poor choice of partitions can drop the failure-detection rate below that of simple random testing (discussed later), while a good choice can significantly improve the failure-detection rate [98, 295].

Symbolic execution is a technique for determining some aspects of program behavior without actually executing the program. In symbolic execution, algebraic symbols are input to a program instead of values. Algebraic expressions describing the transformation of inputs into outputs can then be derived [46]. Clearly, there is a problem of scalability, in that the algebraic expression for a million-line application may be too complicated to be of any use. In addition, symbolic execution cannot represent some very important dynamic behaviors, such as referencing array elements whose index depends on an input variable [147]. Nonetheless, symbolic execution is used as a code analysis tool in a number of publications; one example is in automated test generation for mutation testing (see below) [216].

Program slicing is not a test methodology *per se.*, but rather a method for simplifying a program. A program slice is a decomposition of a program based on dataflow and control flow analysis. Slices are constructed by deleting statements from the original program, to arrive at a reduced program that still behaves identically to the original on a given subset of statements and variables. In essence, a slice is a projection operator applied to source code [293]. Slices are useful in debugging because they promote a clearer understanding of the program for a human tester. Some matters relating to the computation of a program slice may be found in [149].

Mutation analysis was first described in a 1978 article [50], and has been a major research focus since that time. Program mutation is defined as the transformation of a program by inserting a known type of fault at random locations in the program code. The mutant program is then tested in parallel with the original program; whenever a difference is observed, the mutant is said to have been "killed" by the test case; this test is then known to detect the type of fault that was injected. There will normally be a large number of mutant programs generated, and the goal is to construct a suite of test cases that will kill them all. The best-known mutation system at this time is the Mothra system developed at Georgia Tech [145], which performs mutation analysis for Fortran programs. Mothra has been criticized for generating too many program mutants (a criticism that applies to other mutation systems as well), and thus being prohibitively slow [78]. There is also the problem of detecting equivalent mutants – mutants programs that are functionally equivalent to the original program. In general, this is an undecideable problem, but some approximate solutions are discussed in [215]. A somewhat different usage of mutation has been promoted by Voas in [84, 290] and others. Voas uses mutation to measure the *testability* of a program, by introducing various mutations at a single point in the program and then determining the proportion of the mutants that are killed. He refers to this as "sensitivity analysis." Other studies following a similar methodology are also reported in [191, 203].

Finally, the generation of test cases from formal specifications has long been interesting to software testers. One example system is the Anna specification language, which inserts assertions (called *annotations*) into an Ada program to aid in documenting and debugging the program [91]. In contrast, [217] offers test criteria designed to automate the process of generating test cases from state-based formal specifications.

The advent of object-oriented technology has profound implications for the software testing process. The basic units of an object-oriented program are classes, which consist of both data and methods that operate on this data. There is thus considerable opportunity for subtle couplings between different methods in a class, through the data elements of that class. In fact, the problem of testing a class very much resembles that problem of testing a procedure-oriented program with a large number of global variables! Couplings also exist between different classes, due to inheritance, containment, or because they are assembled together into components [12, 13]. Integration testing is thus a continuous part of testing object-oriented software, *even at the unit-test level.*

### 2.3.2 Black-Box Testing

Black-box testing refers to testing techniques that assume no knowledge of the detailed structure of a program. The two most prominent black-box approaches are functional testing and random testing. Functional testing examines whether or not the software conforms to its specifications, without regard to the internal structure of a program. User acceptance tests always take this form, and it is also useful for developers. In particular, testing to ensure that the software correctly processes different parts of its input and output domains is an important black-box activity [232].

Random testing was originally considered a very bad idea. Software engineers considered it to be the least structured and least effective means of testing a program. Black box testing was thought to be superior, and white box testing better still [65]. However, studies in [65] and [66] showed that randomly selecting inputs was a viable alternative to generating test suites based on white-box coverage criteria. A larger number of test cases have to be generated in the random-testing approach, but this cost was offset by the ease with which a test case was generated compared to the white-box approaches. Furthermore, random testing is an essential component of reliability analysis. The structured approach of white-box testing does not produce statistically valid data for reliability analysis; only randomly selected inputs, drawn from a distribution representing the anticipated use of the software (the *operational profile*) produce valid reliability data [123, 207]. Thus, random testing is now considered a crucial part of any systems test plan.

### 2.3.3 Testing Graphical User Interfaces

A Graphical User Interface (GUI) is an intuitive, visual means of interacting with a computer system. GUI systems are used extensively in almost every area of computing; prominent examples include the Windows® and Macintosh® operating systems. GUI systems are event-driven, which means that they respond to user inputs as they arrive, rather than scripting a user's interaction through command lines or hierarchical menus [185, 186]. Most GUI systems use the WIMP interface style, an acronym for Windows, Icons, Menus, and Pointers. The different elements of the WIMP interface are known as widgets; a single GUI may have dozens of widgets in use at any time, each displayed as a bitmap. The user is able to manipulate these widgets in the virtual environment of the computer desktop, and those manipulations translate directly into commands to the computer system. Window widgets are usually top-level widgets, which act as terminals in their own right. Subordinate widgets are attached to the window to provide functionality. Icon widgets are small pictures that represent some system element; they could be inactive windows, disk drives, individual files, etc. Menu widgets provide a choice of services that the GUI is able to provide, in a familiar format (whole interfaces can be built on menus alone, such as an ATM screen). Finally, the pointer widget is a cursor controlled by an input device such as a mouse or trackball. The pointer indicates the location on the virtual desktop where any event will be focussed [55].

The event-driven nature of GUI programs, combined with the size and complexity of the GUI itself, makes them extremely difficult to test. Consider a typical 1024×768 desktop; this interface consists of a variety of bitmaps scattered arbitrarily over a virtual desktop having more than 3/4 of a million pixels. A user of this GUI is able to present an enormous number of distinct inputs to the system, each of which must be caught, parsed, and acted upon. The amount of code dedicated to operating just the GUI itself might be 50-60% of the entire program [185]. Some of the main difficulties in testing GUI programs include establishing test coverage criteria, automatically generating test cases, creating automated oracles for a GUI, and determining what test cases can or should be re-used during regression testing. Very little automated support for these tasks is available; most of the tools currently in use are just record-playback systems that record a user's actions as a script. A dissertation on automated GUI testing by Dr. Atif Memon was completed in 2001, in which automated planning algorithms were used to select test cases for a GUI system [185].

## 2.4 Artificial Intelligence in Software Testing

Much like automatic programming, automatic debugging has long been a major research initiative for the AI community. A 1998 survey [276] divides the automatic debugging field into two categories: tutorial systems and diagnostic systems. Tutorial systems are intended to assist novice programmers, and can only consider fairly basic problems. The systems will attempt to match a student's program against a library of example programs, thus determining what the student intended to do. The systems have to be able to cope with distortions introduced by bugs in the student's program, and indicate to the student where the program fault lies. Diagnostic systems, on the other hand, are intended to assist professional software developers in debugging complex software. Obviously, such systems cannot rely on a stored library of examples. Instead, model-based reasoning is employed. A system model is developed from the specifications of a software system, and the behavior of this model is compared against the actual behavior of the software system for a given test case. Differences imply that a program error exists. However, there is a difference between model-based diagnosis for hardware and software systems. In a hardware system, the specification is the correct description of the system, and any discrepancies between the actual system and the model imply an implementation error. In software systems, the specifications themselves are frequently in error;

thus, a discrepancy between the system and model outputs on a test case may very well reflect a specification error or omission. Determining whether the specification or the implementation is at fault remains a non-trivial task [276].

A large amount of work has also gone into developing AI tools for automatic test case generation. One fairly intuitive representation of programs is as systems of constraints. If this view is adopted, then constraint-solving techniques may be used to generate test cases. This approach is described in [89], where constraint solving was used to detect the existence or absence of a feasible control path passing through some arbitrary point in a program's control graph. If such a path exists, a test input to execute that path is generated. The one real deficiency of [89] is a very common problem: the example used to illustrate the procedure is trivial in size (a total of 15 statements), and so we cannot say how the technique will perform when scaled up to a commercial-sized program.

An important AI technique for generating test cases is automatic partial-order planning. A partial-order planner is an AI technique for generating a sequence of steps to solve a problem. A partial-order planner needs to be given an initial state (the problem), a goal state (the solved problem), and a set of operators that can be used to alter a problem state. Given these tools, the planner will begin generating a partially-ordered set of operations that reduce the difference between a current problem state and the goal state, beginning at the initial state. The partially-ordered operations can then be linearized; any linearization that does not violate the ordering constraints among the operations is then a solution to the problem [256]. AI planners were used to generate test cases for a robotic tape library system in [179, 259].

Finally, the development of a testing agent system is described in [38]. An agent is a persistent, autonomous software entity that exists for a specific purpose. Agent architectures can often be designed as a cooperating community of individual agents, working together to solve a problem (and thus having "social" capabilities). The agent system in [38] consists of three agents: an agent for communicating with a human tester, an agent for generating test cases, and an agent for conducting regression testing. The three agents employ a rule-based knowledge representation scheme to reason about their activities.

## 2.5 Computational Intelligence in Software Testing

Computationally intelligent systems are also used for test-case generation. The key to this usage is a formulation of the test-case selection problem as an optimization problem, which can then be solved by genetic algorithms, simulated annealing, or other optimization algorithms. The first attempt to cast test case selection as an optimization problem was made by Miller and Spooner in [198], in which the authors developed a method for selecting test cases for floating-point operations. They set every integer and conditional value to some arbitrary constant, in order to drive execution down a selected path. They then used a numerical optimization scheme to select the floating-point inputs to the system. This technique was never widely used, since the manual overhead of pre-specifying every integer value and conditional is quite high. However, a second paper on using optimization *has* been quite useful; this is Korel's dynamic execution technique [147]. The dynamic execution technique actually executes the program under test while searching for test cases, in contrast to symbolic execution. By actually executing the program, the old problems from symbolic execution – such as array references that depend on an input variable – are avoided. Returning to the example of Figure 2.1 (from which the control flow graph of Figure 2.2 was computed), one of the possible paths through this program is $P = (1,2,3,4,5,7,9,10,11)$. Korel's technique is to associate a function with each branch point. If an input follows the selected path at each branch point, then this function is 0 at each branch; otherwise, it is a positive value at each non-conforming branch, determined by the branch condition. By minimizing these functions, subject to the constraint that the selected path is followed, an input which will force the program to follow the selected path is selected.

Korel chose to use a direct-search technique in [147], and extended this technique to account for subroutines in [148]; quite obviously, other techniques could also be used. For example, the GADGET (Genetic

Algorithm Data GEneration Tool) described in [193] uses a genetic algorithm for just this purpose. The GADGET tool was also extended to permit the use of gradient descent, simulated annealing, and a differential genetic algorithm in [192]. Tracey, Clark and Mander [284] use a simulated annealing algorithm to solve the optimization problem, while genetic algorithms are again used in [225, 285].

Three other papers that have a different take on using computational intelligence in software testing should also be mentioned. In [3], a genetic algorithm was used to find timing errors in an embedded system for the power generation industry. The genetic algorithm was used to find test cases that forced the system towards longer processing times, in order to cause a violation of the system's timing constraints. The genetic algorithm was considerably superior to a random test-generation scheme in this instance. In [86], the authors tackle the very important question of when to stop testing software. This question is usually approached through the use of software reliability models, such as we discuss in Chapter 3. The authors of [86] instead look for a fuzzy function (i.e. a function of fuzzy numbers) to serve as a reliability function. Since this function is deterministic, it can be solved using numerical optimization techniques, yielding the optimal release time for the software. Finally, neural networks were used to create automated software oracles in [289]. Test oracles automatically determine whether the output of a software system is correct or not, based on a model of the software system. They are extremely important in the automated testing of large software systems, since manually executing a single test case to determine the correct output is a time consuming task that does not scale up to the huge test suites needed for modern software. In [289], a neural network was trained to mimic a software system, and then detect any changes in behavior when the software system was modified.

## 2.6 Remarks

A large amount of research has been directed at the problem of testing software in the last 40 years. The goal of this research is always the improvement of software quality; that is, engineers seek ways to reveal as many program faults as possible before the program is shipped to a customer. The difficulty of this effort cannot be overstated; software systems are becoming more and more complex, as developers seek to take advantage of the explosive improvement in computer hardware. Jones [122] reports that the very largest software systems (the enterprise systems developed by SAP and others) are now reaching 500,000 function points in size. Automated testing support has now become absolutely vital to the software industry, and artificial intelligence approaches can be a very useful part of automated testing. Memon's recent development of an AI planning system for GUI testing [185] is a very important contribution, as are the genetic algorithms discussed in Section 2.5. However, testing by itself is simply not sufficient; engineers cannot hope to visit even a significant fraction of the possible states of a large software system. It is clear from the discussion in this chapter that testing techniques cannot provide assurance that a software system is correct, and so alternative mechanisms to infer the reliability and quality of a software system are required.

In the next three chapters of this book, we present experimental work concerning just such alternative mechanisms. In Chapter 3, we take a fresh look at software reliability modeling, and investigate nonlinear determinism and chaos as an alternative mechanism to create software reliability models. By examining three software reliability datasets using nonlinear time series analysis, we will show that a nonlinear deterministic process appears to be a superior explanation to stochastic processes for the dynamic behaviors in these datasets. This result has significant implications for software reliability modeling; it shows that the stochastic models normally used in software reliability models may not be representative of the actual uncertainty present in software reliability data; the data may be *irregular* rather than random. In Chapters 4 and 5, software quality models based on software metrics are examined. Intriguingly, the literature on using computational intelligence and machine learning to develop such models has two significant holes: the well-known fuzzy c-means algorithm has never been used in this area, and the technique of *resampling* a dataset to correct for skewness is also absent. Accordingly, a fuzzy cluster analysis of 3 software metrics datasets is described in chapter 4, and a resampling technique applied to these three datasets in chapter 5. The outcome of these two chapters is a practical suggestion for using machine learning and resampling techniques in conjunction with a system prototype. An automated filter for recognizing potentially failure-prone system modules in the context of a given project is suggested as an addition to current software development processes.

# Chapter 3

# Chaos Theory and Software Reliability

## 3.1 Introduction

Reliability, in the general engineering sense, is *the probability that a given component or system in a given environment will operate correctly for a specified period of time*. Notice that this definition means that reliability is dependent on the environment in which a component or system is placed, and how long the period of observation is. In general, the longer a system is running, the greater the chance of failure becomes. Placing a system in a different environment could increase or decrease the chance of a failure occurring [162]. Software reliability is defined as *the probability that a given software system in a given environment will operate correctly for a specified period of time.* As part of the software engineering process, developers attempt to gauge the reliability of their software, and compare the current level of reliability with the past history of that software. If a software system is experiencing fewer failures as time goes on, the reliability of that system is said to be growing. This is obviously the desired situation; software that is experiencing an increasing number of failures as time proceeds is a project manager's nightmare. Assuming a project is experiencing reliability growth, two questions have to be answered: when should the software be shipped, and what will its reliability be at that time? These questions are answered by the use of software reliability models [174].

A basic assumption in software reliability modeling is that software failures are the result of a stochastic process, having an unknown probability distribution. Software reliability models (e.g. [88, 117, 206]) specify some reasonable form for this distribution, and are fitted to data from a software project. Once a model demonstrates a good fit to the available data, it can be used to determine the current reliability of the software, and predict the reliability of the software at future times [174]. The central question in this chapter is, *why* are software failures modeled as stochastic processes? After all, no software developer rolls a set of dice and says "Aha! Time to make a mistake!" Unlike failures in hardware systems, where the random occurrence of material defects is unavoidable, *every software failure is the result of a human mistake.*

Randomness is a particular kind of uncertainty, one that is properly modeled by probability theory. It is the species of uncertainty concerned with events that follow the *law of large numbers.* This law is based on the idea that there is an underlying "true" probability distribution with mean μ for some experiment or phenomenon. The law of large numbers states that as you repeatedly perform the experiment or sample the phenomenon, the sample mean will converge to μ for an infinite number of samples [249]. However, other kinds of uncertainty exist, for which probabilistic models are *not* appropriate. For instance, the uncertainty present in human language, commonly referred to as "vagueness," is not random in nature. It is, in fact, just imprecision, and can be represented by fuzzy sets [146]. Our investigation in this chapter centers on experimentally determining what form of uncertainty is present in three sets of software reliability data; is the data drawn from a stochastic process, or is another mechanism at work?

There does not seem to be a mechanism for bringing the law of large numbers into play in software reliability experiments. Previous authors have offered a few qualitative statements to support their treatment of time-to-failure or number of failures as a random variable. These are usually limited to a few sentences in the introduction to a paper. The arguments used include the statement by Musa that "Since the number of failures occurring in infinite time is dependent on the specific history of execution of a program, it is best viewed as a random variable..." [209] or simply the assumption that "The life lengths of the software at each stage of development are random variables..." [180]. A more specific assertion, due to Musa [206], is that while a programmer may not make errors randomly, the location of errors in the code is random, and the test case inputs applied to the software are random. The latter point has been extensively criticized. Littlewood [171], Schneidewind [260], and Cai, Wen and Zhang [33] have all pointed out that test cases are *not* randomly selected, but rather are chosen based on some test plan. This eliminates one obvious source of randomness, although during specific periods of *reliability* testing (as opposed to just debugging), test inputs will be selected at random (see Chapter 2). The well-known relationship between module complexity and module failures [67, 167] is further evidence that the locations of faults in source code are not random. Littlewood goes on to assert that failures do not follow a probability distribution as such; he argues for the use of Bayesian inference instead [171]. In a similar vein, Cai, Wen and Zhang argue that there is no repeated sampling of a phenomenon in software testing, and hence the law of large numbers is irrelevant [33]. They argue for the use of fuzzy set theory to represent the uncertainty present in software reliability. The entire debate over randomness in the literature has been conducted via qualitative statements; there is no hard evidence favoring one point of view over another. The main result of this chapter is a statistical test of the hypothesis that software failures arise from a stochastic process; these results indicate that failures are likely the result of a complicated deterministic process, rather than a stochastic process.

Software failures ultimately arise from mistakes in the program's source code, mistakes that are made by human beings. Human mistakes in general do not appear to be random events; more specifically, there is no probability distribution that has been shown to govern when a programmer will make an error. Instead, the infrequent and unpredictable occurrence of human errors seems to more closely resemble the form of uncertainty known as irregularity. This form of uncertainty is qualitatively different from randomness, and incorporates such phenomena as intermittency, bifurcations and rare events. Irregularity is best modeled by chaos theory and fractal sets, in the same way that randomness is best modeled by probability theory. This work is in accordance with a basic tenet of CI: that there are different forms of uncertainty, and when they are encountered, the appropriate modeling technique must be employed [223]. The causal model for software failures we propose is that faults are irregularly distributed in the input space of a program. More specifically, it is hypothesized that the subset of the input space which will trigger a fault (the *fault set*) is a fractal set [84, 152]. The uncertain nature of software failures is thus a result of the peculiar geometry of fractal sets, instead of any inherent randomness. In order to directly test this hypothesis, it is necessary to reconstruct the complete fault set of a program, which is impossible given the nature of the datasets under study. However, an implication of this hypothesis is that a time series of software failure occurrences will show evidence of deterministic behavior. Since the software reliability datasets under study consist of exactly this type of data, testing for this implication is the main focus of this chapter. Finding evidence of deterministic behavior in these datasets will indirectly support the hypothesis of a fractal fault set, and will directly demonstrate that irregularity is an important feature of software reliability growth

Nonlinear time series analysis is the name given to a collection of techniques for analyzing time series data, which are based on chaos theory. In nonlinear time series analysis, low dimensional chaos is used as an alternative explanation to linear stochastic processes in modeling and forecasting complex signals. This alternative implies that a deterministic process is the basis of the time series, rather than a random process, and that deterministic models should perform better in predicting reliability growth for software systems. However, the sensitivity to initial conditions displayed by chaotic systems means that this predictability is limited to a short time frame, beyond which any prediction scheme becomes useless. The main problem in nonlinear time series analysis is that the theorems on which these techniques are based assume an infinite amount of data. The limitations of finite time series make is possible for undifferentiated white noise to sometimes appear to come from a low-dimensional chaotic system. Considerable effort is thus devoted to noise reduction, to ensuring that the time series under examination are stationary, and to removing temporal correlations (which can also be mistaken for chaotic dynamics) [130].

Three software reliability datasets have been analyzed using the nonlinear time series techniques described in [130] and implemented in [103]. One of these datasets was collected by Musa [45], while the remaining two are originally from IBM, and were obtained from [174].

These datasets are plotted in Figures 3.1-3.3. In these figures, the *x*-axis represents the *i*-th failure, and the *y*-axis represents the elapsed time between the (*i*-1)-th failure and the *i*-th failure (the *interfailure* time). Viewed in this form, the time series exhibit some very irregular behavior, and show a considerable amount of structure. However, a nonlinear test reveals that the datasets are indeed stationary. Since the software systems underlying these datasets were undergoing constant change, one would expect to see evidence of nonstationary behavior. However, regression testing is not included in these datasets, and hence the test cases that caused failures are not actually revisited. Thus, the datasets are effectively stationary. Clear evidence of deterministic behavior has been found in these datasets, which was quantified using a standard technique in nonlinear time series analysis, known as surrogate data. Various analytical probability distributions have been fitted to the datasets, but the Kolomogorov-Smirnoff goodness-of-fit test indicates that none of these distributions actually represent the data. These results indicate that the standard assumption of an underlying stochastic process is inadequate for these datasets.

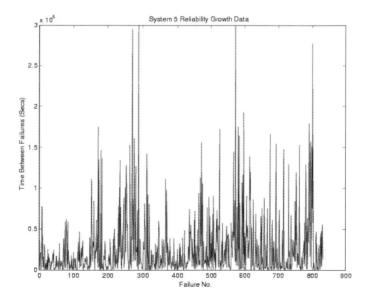

Figure 3.1: Reliability Growth Data for System 5

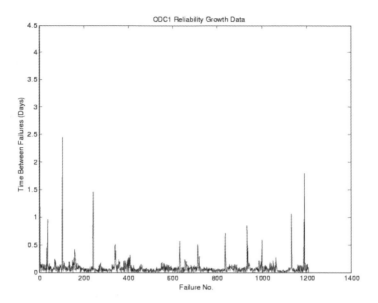

Figure 3.2: Reliability Growth Data from ODC1

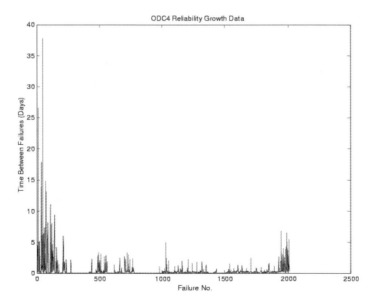

Figure 3.3: Reliability Growth Data from ODC4

In Section 2 of this chapter, concepts from hardware and software reliability engineering, and previous work in software reliability modeling are reviewed. The nonlinear time series analysis techniques used in this investigation, and the specific characteristics of the datasets, are presented in Section 3, and Section 4 is devoted to the experimental results of this investigation and their significance.

## 3.2 Reliability Engineering for Software

This section is devoted to a review of reliability engineering, as applied to both hardware and software systems. First, an overview of reliability engineering in general and the special challenges of determining the reliability of a software system is provided. These challenges arise from the fact that software is logical entity, rather than a physical object. The rich variety of software reliability models will then be discussed.

### 3.2.1 Reliability Engineering

Reliability engineering is the discipline of scientifically estimating how well a technological system will perform its intended function. Reliability engineering cuts across all the traditional disciplines of engineering; after all, whether engineers are building a bridge, a jet airplane, or a hydraulic valve, they must eventually be able to quantify how long this system will perform correctly. Technically, reliability is defined as the probability that a given technological system, in a given operating environment, will fulfill its intended function for a given period of time [162]. There is a close connection between reliability and quality. In the popular mind, they may be one and the same. After all, a quality product is one that does what it's supposed to do, when the user wants it done. However, in quality control, reliability is viewed as an attribute of a product, while quality can be considered the degree of excellence of the product when *all* attributes of the product are considered [92]. Reliability is also closely allied with safety; where reliability engineering is concerned with product defects that can cause a failure, safety engineering is concerned with those product failures that may create a hazard to life, limb or property. As an example, consider an automated tram, such as may be found at many airports around the U.S. A number of attributes will contribute to the quality of this system; one such could be the maximum change of acceleration experienced by passengers. A rough ride will create a perception of poor quality, while a smooth ride will indicate higher quality. The reliability engineer, on the other hand, is concerned about the possibility of failures. What, for instance, is the probability that the tram will become stuck at a station, or even worse, between two stations? The safety engineer is concerned about failures that might create a danger to passengers or property, such as failing to stop before the tram hits an end wall [162].

While reliability is a crucial attribute of any technological system, it is still only one of a number of design parameters an engineer must keep in mind. The most reliable car in the world will sit forever in a dealer's lot if it costs a million dollars and reaches a top speed of 45 miles per hour. Cost, performance, and reliability are necessary and conflicting requirements for any product. Much of the art of engineering design involves balancing these conflicting demands [162].

3.2.1.1 Reliability Analysis

The reliability of a technological system is not the same at every moment of the system's lifetime. In fact, three distinct "epochs" can be observed in most systems: the infancy period, normal operation, and wear-out. The infancy epoch is the time period immediately following the system's manufacture and installation. For most technological systems, this is a critical period, during which design & manufacturing flaws will come to light and cause a failure. This circumstance is referred to as an "infant mortality" failure. During routine operation, failures are normally the result of chance events in the system's environment, and are not time-dependent. Unexpected external events are the prime source of failures during this time period. Near the end of the useful life of a system, parts age and wear out, leading to a sharp increase in the number of failures. These wear-out failures signal the need to replace the system, and mark the end of the system's lifetime. A pictorial representation of this discussion can be created by graphing the expected failure rate of a system with respect to time, as in Figure 3.4. This idealized "bathtub" curve is typical of most technological systems [162].

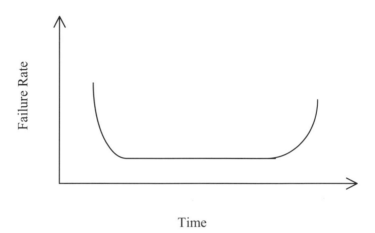

Time

Figure 3.4: System Failures Rates Over Time

Formally, a system's reliability, its failure rate, and the Mean Time To Failure (MTTF) are related in the following manner [162]. Treat the running time of a system as a random variable, denoted by $T$, and define the following probability density function

$$f(t) = P\{t < T \le t + \Delta t\} \tag{3.1}$$

as the probability that a failure occurs in the interval $[t,t+\Delta t]$ for vanishingly small $\Delta t$. This gives the cumulative density function

$$F(t) = \int_{-\infty}^{t} f(t)dt \text{ or } F(t) = P\{T \le t\} \tag{3.2}$$

where $F(t)$ represents the probability that a failure occurs before time $t$. Since the definition of reliability is the probability that a failure does *not* occur before time $t$, the reliability function is

$$R(t) = 1 - F(t) \qquad (3.3)$$

As boundary conditions, $R(0) = 1$ and $R(\infty) = 0$.

The failure rate and the MTTF may be determined from the reliability function and the failure PDF. The failure rate $\lambda(t)$ is the probability that the system will fail during the interval $[t, t+\Delta t]$ given that the system does not fail before time $t$. This may be expressed in terms of the failure PDF and the reliability function as

$$\lambda(t) = \frac{f(t)}{R(t)} \qquad (3.4)$$

The failure rate is also often referred to as the hazard rate or mortality rate. The MTTF, as its name implies, is just the expected value of the failure time $t$, yielding

$$MTTF = \int_0^\infty tf(t)dt, \qquad (3.5a)$$

or equivalently [162],

$$MTTF = \int_0^\infty R(t)dt \qquad (3.5b)$$

Thus far, the form of $f(t)$, the failure PDF, has not been specified. Obviously, knowing $f(t)$ is crucial to any reliability analysis. However, given the sheer complexity of technological systems and the world with which they interact, knowing the "true" form of $f(t)$ is an unrealistic goal. Instead, reasonable approximations are used, based on assumptions about the system's behavior over time. For instance, if infant mortality and aging can be neglected, then only random failures occurring during normal operation are of any concern. Since these are time-independent, the failure rate is constant. This leads to the exponential distribution as a form for $f(t)$:

$$f(t) \approx \alpha e^{-\alpha t} \tag{3.6}$$

From this the reliability function and MTTF are

$$R(t) = e^{-\alpha t} \tag{3.7}$$

$$MTTF = \frac{1}{\alpha} \tag{3.8}$$

The exponential distribution is only appropriate for modeling a constant failure rate. In order to include infant mortality or aging, other distributions must be used. The most common are the normal, the lognormal, and the Weibull distributions. The normal distribution is appropriate when an expected time-to-failure is known, along with a confidence interval for that time-to-failure. The lognormal is useful in the similar situation when an estimated failure time is known, along with a factor n that plays a similar role to a confidence interval, i.e. some degree of confidence that the true failure time lies in the interval $[t/n, nt]$ can be obtained [162].

One of the most widely used distributions in reliability analysis is the Weibull distribution. If the number of failures over time obeys a power law, then this distribution can be very useful. The failure rate is assumed to follow the power law

$$\lambda(t) = \frac{m}{\theta} \left( \frac{t}{\theta} \right)^{m-1} \tag{3.9}$$

This yields the failure PDF

$$f(t) = \frac{m}{\theta}\left(\frac{t}{\theta}\right)^{m-1}\exp\left[-\left(\frac{t}{\theta}\right)^m\right]$$     (3.10)

and the CDF and reliability are

$$F(t) = 1 - \exp\left[-\left(\frac{t}{\theta}\right)^m\right]$$     (3.11)

$$R(t) = \exp\left[-\left(\frac{t}{\theta}\right)^m\right]$$     (3.12)

The Weibull is an extremely flexible distribution; in [162], Lewis shows how the bathtub curve of Figure 3.4 could be approximated by the superposition of three Weibull curves. However, this flexibility comes at a price. Closed-form expressions for the MTTF are difficult to obtain, and no closed-form solution exists for the maximum-likelihood estimates of the parameters $m$ and $\theta$ [244].

For many technological systems, the first failure is also the last. However, some systems *can* be repaired after they fail; these are known as *repairable* systems. For repairable systems, the MTTF remains an important quantity. However, the probability of the system being operational at any given time, and the average time to repair the system, now become important quantities as well. These are referred to as the *availability* and the *Mean Time to Repair* (MTTR), respectively. Availability is simply defined as the probability that the system is operational at time $t$. A related quantity is the *steady-state availability* $A(\infty)$, which represents the system availability after some initial failures have occurred. To define the MTTR, begin by defining the *maintainability* of the system. Let the time required to repair a failure be a random variable T, and define the PDF $m(t)$ to be

$$m(t) = P\{t \le T \le t + \Delta t\}$$     (3.13)

The maintainability of the system is defined as the corresponding CDF $M(t)$. The MTTR is then the expected value of $m(t)$:

$$MTTR = \int_0^\infty tm(t)dt \qquad (3.14)$$

A key point about repairs is that they are made by humans, and are thus subject to a wide variation of skill, experience, training, diligence, and even day-to-day performance. Thus, it is much more difficult to fit a distribution for $m(t)$. Since the availability of a system is contingent on both the MTTF and MTTR of the system, this means that estimating the steady state availability is quite difficult. However, if we presume that the MTTR is relatively constant, the approximation

$$A(\infty) = \frac{MTTF}{MTTF + MTTR} \qquad (3.15)$$

can be used to represent the steady-state availability of a system [162].

### 3.2.1.2 Reliability Testing

All engineering analysis is based on scientifically gathered data, and reliability engineering is no different. The collection of reliability data is referred to as reliability testing. There are two distinct forms of reliability testing, each with its own procedures and goals. *Reliability Growth Testing* is conducted to find and remove the causes of failure in a technological system, while *Life Testing* attempts to determine the useful life of that technological system. Common to both forms of testing is the constraint of cost; if an expensive system must be tested to destruction to obtain a single observation, obtaining a statistically valid sample may be prohibitively expensive. Time is also a constraint, since products must be shipped within a reasonable amount of time. Failure analysis, censoring, and acceleration are techniques used in reliability testing to overcome these constraints [162].

Reliability growth testing is typically conducted on system prototypes, before the design is frozen. The goal of this form of testing is to reveal the system's failure modes, so that they may be eliminated by a design change. A system prototype is activated, and run until it fails. The time of this failure (the running time until the failure occurred) is recorded. After each failure is observed, the failure is analyzed and its cause determined. The product is then repaired, and the cause of that failure is removed. The prototype is then reactivated, and run until the next failure is observed, and the cycle repeats. The $n$ failure times $t_i$ $(i = 1, 2, ..., n)$ constitute the reliability growth data for this system. There appears to be a power-law relationship between the number of failures and the total running time for the system (the sum of the $t_i$'s):

$$n(T) = e^b T^{1-\alpha} \qquad (3.16)$$

where $n(T)$ is the number of failures occurring by time $T$ and $T = \sum t_i$. Reliability growth data will normally continue to be gathered even after a system goes into operational use, both to refine the system and to set maintenance policies [162].

Life testing, unlike reliability growth testing, explicitly requires the use of multiple copies of a technological system. The individual systems are run until they fail, and from this data an estimate of the expected lifetime of the system in service is obtained. However, it is usually infeasible to wait for all the copies of the system to fail, and sometimes the predicted service life of the system is so long that waiting for even *one* copy to fail naturally is unacceptable. The techniques used to overcome these constraints are censoring and accelerated testing. Censoring is the removal of some copies of a system from the test before they actually fail, or because their failure occurs under circumstances that do not affect the expected lifetime of the system. Censoring is a better option than simply deleting the removed unit from the test entirely, since there is valuable information available from those units up until the time they are removed [162].

Pressures on the design team to end testing early come from economic factors; there is a need to put the system into production before market conditions render it unprofitable. Those same pressures make it even more difficult to test systems whose design life is very long. In those cases, it is not practical to wait for the length of time it would take for even one copy of the system to fail under normal use. In these cases, accelerated life testing is used to obtain usable estimate of the life expectancy of the system. Acceleration is a technique for compressing the operational life of a system into a much smaller period of calendar time than would ordinarily be required. The simplest form of acceleration is compressed-time testing, which can be used on systems that do not run continuously throughout their lives. By running these systems continuously instead of intermittently, we can obtain an estimate of their life expectancy in much less time than would ordinarily be required. Likewise, start-up failures can be accelerated by constantly starting and stopping the system. For those systems that run continuously, a technique called advanced-stress testing can be used. The system is subjected to a greater load or a harsher environment than it would ordinarily encounter, which should lead to an increased failure rate. If a quantitative relationship between the increased stress and reduced operating life can be established, then an estimate of the true life expectancy can be generated [162].

### 3.2.2 Software Reliability Engineering

The integration of software reliability engineering into the software development life-cycle must go considerably beyond just testing the product. For example, a study of best current practices for software reliability engineering was completed at AT&T in the early nineties [70]. Twenty process activities were identified that were necessary for integrating software reliability into the development cycle; the activities began in the feasibility and requirements studies, and continued right through the deployment and maintenance phases. In the feasibility and requirements phase, the expected operational usage of the software must be specified, and what constitutes a failure must be defined. The trade-off between cost and reliability must then be determined. During design and implementation, the overall reliability objective must be decomposed into component reliabilities, and each component must be designed and implemented to meet its allocated reliability. During systems test, reliability growth testing is carried out, and eventually the product is certified as having met its reliability objectives. When the system is mission-ready, its field performance and customer satisfaction must be tracked, and any evolution of the software must be certified to meet the original system reliability goal. Another recommendation in [43] is to employ statistical designs during the testing phase, rather than relying solely on the tester's judgment to decide what test cases should be run. A standard for software reliability engineering has been jointly authored by the American National Standards Institute (ANSI) and the American Institute of Aeronautics and Astronautics (AIAA) [4].

Software reliability engineering is based on the collection of reliability growth data. Plainly, the debugging cycle of finding, analyzing and fixing software faults yields precisely this type of data. The data collected during this cycle is usually the amount of time that the software has operated since the last failure, *excluding* regression testing. Regression testing consists of re-running test cases that the system passed before a change was made; the goal is to determine if that change has degraded the reliability of the system. Regression testing data is not useful as reliability data, because it is not randomly selected; the choice of what subset of previous test cases to use as a regression test suite is an important economic choice, as they will not reveal new faults, only potential faults related to the repair of a known fault. Life testing, on the other hand, is not conducted in software reliability engineering. The reason for this goes back to the logical nature of software; unlike physical systems, which exist in the analog world, digital information like software can be copied perfectly, every time. Thus, there is no variation between copies of a software system, and no need to estimate the expected lifetime of the software. The time required for one copy to fail will be the exact time required for each copy to fail, given identical inputs and environments.

Another significant difference between hardware reliability and software reliability may be observed in the failure rates of hardware and software systems. The failure rate of a system normally changes over time. Hardware systems typically exhibit the behavior shown in Figure 3.4. The typical failure rate of a software system, on the other hand, will have a general form similar to Figure 3.5. As with hardware systems, there is an initial region in which the failure rate decreases sharply, corresponding to system testing and debugging. After this, there is a fairly constant failure rate, corresponding to system usage. However, there is no final region of increasing failures, because *software does not wear out*. Software, being a logical entity, is not subject to wear and environmental degradation. A piece of software is as capable of fulfilling its *original* mission thirty, forty or fifty years after it was installed as it was on the first day it was operational. Note, however, that this neglects the effect of maintenance and enhancement activities on the software. Systems that undergo extensive maintenance and enhancement do experience reliability decay, as errors made by the maintenance and enhancement teams accumulate over time [87, 174].

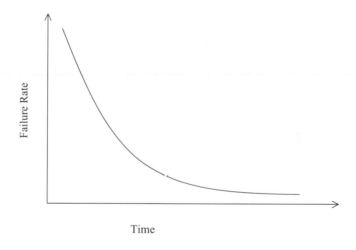

Figure 3.5: Software Failure Rates Over Time

One area in which hardware and software systems seem to be similar is in their response to an increased load. Reliability engineers have long known that when a system is placed under an increased load, the system will fail more often. Furthermore, this failure response need not be linearly related to the load increase [162]. In this context, the work of Iyer and Rossetti [114] is very important, because it establishes a similar behavior for software systems. The authors studied the performance of the operating system of an IBM 3081 at the Stanford Linear Accelerator Center, and found that the number of failures was correlated with the volume of interactive processing (paging rate, operating system CPU time, etc.), but was not correlated with the overall CPU usage. This indicates that "loads" for a software system are interactive operations, and not compute-bound processes.

Other experimental investigations of software failures have been conducted, especially at NASA. Dunham reports on fault characterization experiments conducted at NASA in the mid-eighties in [62]; follow-up experiments in the late eighties and early nineties are reported in [63, 76]. The latter reference also establishes two characteristics of software faults: first, individual faults seem to be associated with contiguous regions of the input space that will trigger them; these were referred to as *error crystals*. Secondly, a log-linear relationship between the failure rate and the number of remaining errors in a software system was described. These two characteristics are very suggestive in the context of the investigation in this chapter. One of the characteristics of a fractal set is that there must be an inverse power-law relationship between the size of elements in a set and elements having at least that size; thus, there will be a few large elements and many smaller ones [178]. Taking the size of a fault to be the hypervolume of the associated error crystal, the hypothesis of a fractal fault set implies that there should be an inverse power-law relationship between the size of a fault and the number of faults having at least that size. The fault detection rate (i.e. failure rate) will initially be very high, but will drop off sharply as the few large faults are found; the numerous smaller faults are much harder to detect. A log-linear relationship between these quantities thus makes intuitive sense. This log-linear behavior contradicts a basic assumption in many popular software reliability models, as will be discussed in the next section.

### *3.2.3 Software Reliability Models*

Once a software system's reliability growth data has been collected, the next step is to fit a probability distribution to this data, and thereby obtain the reliability function, failure rate, and mean time to failure for the software. Such a distribution is known as a software reliability growth model (SRGM), and they play a key role in software development. Used judiciously, they help determine when a software system may be released into the marketplace, and how reliable that system is. The history of software reliability models goes back to the early 1970s, and continues to be an active research area today. The first software reliability model to gain widespread acceptance was the Jelinski-Moranda de-eutrophication model [117]. The authors discussed the state of the art in software reliability research in the year 1971; some of their comments are still depressingly applicable today. Their model assumed that the failure rate of a software system at any time is proportional (instead of log-linear) to the number of errors remaining in the software at that time. Maximum likelihood estimates for the two parameters of the model are developed, and the model is tested on real-world software failure data (in this case, trouble reports from a U.S. Navy combat information system). This paper sets a pattern that most software reliability papers follow: certain assumptions about software failures are discussed, a model is developed along with any necessary estimation procedures, and then the model is applied to a real-world dataset(s). Forman and Singpurwalla [80] discuss the question of when to stop testing and how to predict whether or not a software system still contains bugs, using the Jelinski-Moranda model as a starting point. Other papers on when to stop testing include [253, 236]. The incorporation of an optimal release time is now a common feature in software reliability papers.

There appear to be three major trends in software reliability research: the use of Non-Homogeneous Poisson Process (NHPP) models, Bayesian inference, and time series analysis. An NHPP is a Poisson process with a time-varying mean value function. This means they are counting processes, having the following characteristics: (i) the total number of failures $N(t) \geq 0$, (ii) $N(t) \in \mathbf{Z}$, (iii) $s < t \Rightarrow N(s) < N(t)$, (iv) $s < t \Rightarrow N(t) - N(s)$ is the number of events occurring in the open interval $(s,t)$, where $\mathbf{Z}$ is the set of integers [251]. An NHPP is governed by the expression

$$P\{N(t) = k\} = \frac{(m(t))^k}{k!} e^{-m(t)} \qquad (3.17)$$

where $N(t)$ is the number of events observed by time $t$, $m(t)$ is the mean value function, and the intensity function is given by the time derivative of $m(t)$ [87]. The use of NHPP models is generally considered to have begun with a paper by Goel and Okumoto [88], although a conference paper using an NHPP was published by Schneidewind [260] in 1975. Like many papers in this field, Jelinski and Moranda's assumption that the failure rate is proportional to the remaining number of errors is incorporated into this model (an assumption that is not supported by the experimental work of [76]). The model also assumes that failures in distinct intervals are independent of each other. These two assumptions are widespread in software reliability modeling, even though authors have criticized them since 1975 [260]. Another very important model is the basic execution-time model developed by Musa [206]. This is probably the most widely used software reliability model today [174]. Musa's model was the first to explicitly use CPU time instead of calendar time as the unit of measurement. In addition, Musa collected a large number of extremely high-quality datasets, which he describes in [206] and which are currently archived at [45]. These datasets have formed the basis for many experimental investigations in the last 20 years. Other NHPP models include the logarithmic Poisson [202, 209, 299, 301]. The development of new NHPP models continues up to the present day; some recent examples are [112, 235].

Bayesian inference in software reliability models essentially consists of treating the parameters of a reliability model as random variables instead of constants to be estimated. Some reasonable prior distributions are assumed for these parameters, and Bayes' theorem is then invoked to determine the posterior distributions using reliability data. The first Bayesian model was presented by Littlewood and Verrall in [172]; the development of Bayesian models continues today, with some examples being [10, 119, 151, 171, 180, 237, 238, 267]. As with the NHPP models, there are a number of assumptions involved in the Bayesian models; a nice illustration of this point may be found in [180], where no less than 8 assumptions are made for "Model I." A most revealing comment is that two of the assumptions were included "...based on mathematical convenience." The inclusion of simplifying assumptions to make the model computationally tractable is common; this has been the source of much criticism of software reliability engineering in the past.

A few papers have used techniques from time series analysis to examine software reliability data. A pair of papers [111, 268] uses a logarithmic transformation of software reliability data. This turns a power law process into a first-order auto-regressive process. The coefficient in this process was allowed to be random, and changing over time. The AR process was then fitted to the transformed data. More recently, Khoshgoftaar and Szabo [142] used an auto-regressive integrated moving average (ARIMA) model. They used both the failure counts and a small number of complexity metrics as regression variables. This is one of the few papers that integrate software reliability modeling with software metrics, even though there is general agreement that the two are related. However, the performance of the model in tracking the original system is actually rather poor; the tracking error oscillates, but the amplitude of those oscillations appears to increase over time. Chaos theory was applied to software reliability modeling by Zou and Li in [309]. The motivation for using chaos theory in that paper was the same as in our current work; they also were not convinced that software failures arise from a stochastic process. However, there are significant methodological problems in [309] The datasets examined in that paper were far too small for use in nonlinear time series analysis, and there was no attempt to account for temporal correlations, non-stationarity, or a test for the presence of deterministic behavior. Zou and Li simply applied the correlation dimension algorithm to three very small datasets, and then created a complex locally linear prediction model for those datasets. In the field of nonlinear time series analysis, this is considered scientifically unsound.

In addition to these three large-scale trends, there have been a great many papers proposing software reliability models that are somewhat unique. Littlewood proposed a semi-Markov process to model the changes of control between modules in a program [170]. The idea in this paper is that transfers of control between modules are failure-prone, much like interfaces between hardware components. Okumoto [220] used the logarithmic Poisson model of [209] to help construct a control chart for software failures. The process has some similarities to the

Shewart control chart, but there is a problem with the predicted values of future failures. When these are plotted with the current set of failures (as in Figure 3 of [220]), all of the predicted values fall on one side of the mean value, indicating a lack of control [92]. Karunanithi and Whitley [132] used a cascade-correlation network to perform one-step-ahead software reliability predictions. If the hypothesis of deterministic behavior in software failures is correct, then this sort of modeling is far more appropriate than stochastic processes. Neural networks were also used for software reliability forecasting in [133]. Kumar, Hariri and Raghavendra [240] extend software reliability concepts to distributed processing systems. They account for different network architecture by integrating graph-theoretic concepts into software reliability studies. Laprie et al. [153] describe a model called the Knowledge-Action-Transformation (KAT) approach, which is based on extending renewal theory to the nonstationary case. The resulting models are extremely complex, and so simplified models are provided for everyday use. Cai, Wen and Zhang [33] develop a software reliability model where the time to failure is a fuzzy number rather than a random variable. Their model is very simple, and incorporates many of the same assumptions found in probabilistic models (i.e. perfect debugging, one fault is removed to fix one error). Kanoun et al. [128] propose combining several existing models into an overall modeling strategy, while Ohba [218] describes two S-shaped reliability models and the hyper-exponential model. A pair of papers describing exponential order statistic models for software reliability may be found in [195, 261].

There have been a number of critical reviews, surveys, and model comparison papers in the software reliability literature. An oft-cited review is Goel's 1985 work [87], which includes a critical review of the underlying assumptions of numerous models. Another review was written by Yamada and Osaki [302]; this includes the logistic and Gompertz curves, which were used for software reliability modeling in Japan for a number of years. Littlewood's 1980 review [171] is also of interest. Musa proposed a classification scheme for software reliability models in [208]; a more up-to-date work making use of this scheme may be found in [73]. Comparative studies of different models may be found in [134, 277].

## 3.3 Nonlinear Time Series Analysis

In this section, the techniques used in analyzing the software reliability datasets, as well as some relevant characteristics of the datasets themselves, are described. An important point that must be acknowledged at the outset is that the data are not particularly well-suited for study using nonlinear methods. None of the three datasets are larger than roughly 2000 elements, and there is considerable discretization noise present in them. Nonlinear time series analysis, on the other hand, demands data of high quality and in large quantity. Data sets on the order of 10000 elements or more are normally used in laboratory experiments, while even the most robust nonlinear analysis algorithms cannot tolerate a noise amplitude of more than 2-3% of the actual signal. The experimental results in this chapter offer firm evidence of deterministic behavior in these time series; while some indications of chaotic behavior were also found, the limitations of the data prevent us from reaching a definitive conclusion about chaos in software reliability data [130].

### *3.3.1 Analytical Techniques*

Kantz and Schrieber [130] is usually cited as the most up-to-date and comprehensive treatise on the use of nonlinear techniques for the analysis of time series data. This investigation applies the results and algorithms developed in [130], and implemented in [103, 262], to the analysis of software reliability data, in which the interfailure times are taken to be a time series. "Time," in these experiments, thus refers to an index of the failures rater than physical time. A delay reconstruction of the phase space of the software system corresponding to each dataset was undertaken, and two-dimensional phase portraits of each system show clear indications (in one case, *dramatic* indications) of deterministic behavior. While this is not scientific evidence, it is reason to continue using the techniques of nonlinear time series analysis in these datasets. Using the method of surrogate data, this evidence was quantified through statistical hypothesis testing. A nonlinear noise reduction algorithm was used to clean the data, and the dimensionality of the phase-space attractor in each dataset was estimated using the correlation dimension technique [130].

A time series is a sequence of scalar measurements over time taken from some interesting system. Information about the underlying system is present in that time series, but extracting it can be a difficult task. The scalar measurements themselves are just a complex projection of the true, unobserved state variables of some system. In order to analyze a system based solely on time-series data, the state space has to be reconstructed. While the *original* state space cannot be uniquely determined, an *equivalent* state space (in the sense that the two are related by a smooth, invertible mapping) can be constructed using the method of delay embeddings. Let a time series with $k$ measurements be denoted by $x_1, x_2, ..., x_k$. A delay embedding of this time series is a sequence of vectors $B_n = (x_{n - (m - 1)v}, x_{n - (m - 2)v}, ..., x_{n - v}, x_n)$. This is an $m$-dimensional vector, formed from successive elements of the original time series. The time lag $v$ takes each consecutive element, every second element, every third element, etc. In general, since delay vectors overlap, a time series of n elements will be converted into a sequence of $n - (m - 1)v$ delay vectors. Another way to look at the time lag is that it increases the time window covered by each vector.

The parameters $m$ and $v$ must be chosen for each time series. Unfortunately, there is no single algorithm that gives the proper values for $m$ and $v$ for any arbitrary data set. One known fact about $m$, the dimension estimate, is that there is a qualitative difference between values of $m$ that are too small, and values that are sufficiently large. If the value for $m$ is smaller than the actual dimension $m_0$, then there will be unresolved projections of the state variables, creating *false neighbors*. For $m > m_0$, these false neighbors do not exist. Thus, searching for false neighbors is a powerful technique for finding a good estimate of $m$. There are no such results for the time lag $v$; mathematically, every choice of $v$ is equivalent to every other choice. From a practical standpoint, however, a proper choice of $v$ helps nonlinear analysis, while a poor choice hinders it. Qualitatively, small values of $v$ make successive delay vectors more and more correlated, so that the phase portrait of the system will be concentrated along the diagonal. Large values of $v$ make the delay vectors virtually uncorrelated, so that they fill a cloud in the phase portrait. The best strategy is to select a promising range for $v$, and then manually inspect each phase portrait. Since noise in the times series denies the analyst access to infinitesimal length scales, the largest possible deterministic structures are desired. Useful hints about promising values of $v$ can be found from the first zero of the autocorrelation function, or from the first minimum of the *time-delayed mutual information* [130].

The phase portrait of a system provides qualitative information about a system. A truly stochastic process will fill a cloud in phase space; deterministic systems with no noise will show clean trajectories. As an example of the latter, consider the Henon map, shown in Figure 3.6. This system is determined by the equations

$$x_{n+1} = a - x_n^2 + by_n$$
$$y_{n+1} = x_n$$

(3.18)

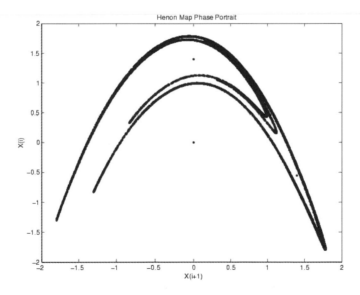

Figure 3.6: The Henon Map

where $a$=1.4 and $b$=0.3 (this choice of parameters induces chaotic behavior in the Henon map [130]). Realistic time series fall somewhere between these two extremes. The appearance of structure in the phase portrait, or even just clear holes, probably signals the presence of deterministic dynamics of some kind. An inspection of the phase portrait of a system is thus a critical first step in analyzing that system.

The algorithms for nonlinear time series analysis all assume that the time series is taken from a stationary process, at a sufficiently high sampling rate. If this assumption is violated, then the algorithms will produce spurious results. Thus, a check for stationarity is needed. In the domain of nonlinear time series, linear statistics such as correlations are not used to test for nonstationarity, as they cannot detect nonlinear relationships. In a number of chaotic systems, parameter drifts may not result in any change of the linear statistics; only nonlinear relationships are affected. Instead, a technique called the space-time separation plot is used [130, 242]. The space-time separation plot creates curves of constant probability for two points to be within a spatial distance of ε of each other, assuming that the time difference is $T$. If these curves saturate in a plateau (or a stable oscillation), then the time series is drawn from a stationary process at an adequate sampling rate. Another way to look at the space-time separation plots is that they show whether or not the time scale of the observations made on a system is sufficiently larger than the internal time scale of the system itself [130].

Once the phase portrait provides an indication that deterministic dynamics are present, and the space-time separation plot shows that the time series is stationary, the next step is to quantify the evidence for determinism through statistical hypothesis testing. The null hypothesis is that the time series is explained by a stochastic process; if the null hypothesis is rejected with at least 95% confidence (significance $\alpha$=0.05), then a scientific basis exists for saying that nonlinear determinism, not randomness, explains the time series. Obviously, this test is rather more involved than the student's t-test! The technique used in the literature is called the method of surrogate data. Essentially, one constructs a group of time series that *are* random in nature, and applies a test statistic that distinguishes between random and deterministic time series (a nonlinear prediction error is a good example). If the original time series has a significantly different value of the statistic from the random sets, then we reject the null hypothesis. The test statistics used in this investigation are the time reversal asymmetry statistic

$$\frac{\left(y_n - y_{n-d}\right)^3}{\left(y_n - y_{n-d}\right)^2} \tag{3.19}$$

and a prediction error obtained from the locally constant noise reduction scheme discussed later [262, 283].

The method of surrogate data was introduced to ensure that the random data sets have the same properties as the original data, but still conform to the hypothesis of random behavior. Essentially, one generates a sequence of random numbers, manipulates that sequence to match a given hypothesis (i.e. that the original data comes from a linear Gaussian process distorted by a nonlinear observation function), and then uses the "polished" sequence as a template for shuffling the original data. This shuffle is then one surrogate data set. Obviously, the surrogate has the same mean and variance as the original data set. One can also ensure that the power spectrum of the surrogate is the same as the original. For a two-sided determinism test, $(2/\alpha) - 1$ surrogates are generated, where $\alpha$ is the desired significance of the test. If the test statistic for the original data is greater or lesser than all the values for the surrogates, the null hypothesis is rejected with significance $\alpha$ [130, 283]. Some authors will reject the null hypothesis if the test statistic for the original data is at least 2.5 standard deviations from the mean of the test statistics for all data sets. However, this assumes that the values of the test statistic are normally distributed, which may be far from the truth [20, 130].

Any realistic time series will be contaminated by noise. This noise is a very serious problem for nonlinear time series analysis. Even the most robust algorithm, the correlation dimension, cannot tolerant a noise amplitude in excess of 2-3% of the total amplitude of the time series [130]. Thus, an important step in nonlinear time series analysis is the use of a nonlinear noise reduction scheme. One such scheme, the locally constant projective scheme, has been described in [130] and implemented in [262]. Assume that a point $X$ in an $m$-dimensional delay embedding has $k$ neighbors within a radius of $\varepsilon$. The next point along the system trajectory passing through $X$ is predicted to be the mean of the one-step evolutions of all $k$ neighbors. This noise reduction technique takes advantage of the property of continuity; trajectories that are initially close will still be close together after a short period of time. Even in chaotic systems, two trajectories that are initially close cannot diverge at more than an exponential rate. This algorithm has been found to be quite robust, and has been applied to a large number of time series [130].

The phase-space attractor of a chaotic system will have a fractal geometry. Fractal sets can exhibit self-similarity, and have a complex structure at all length scales. The geometry of a fractal set is in fact so unique that they can have a noninteger dimensionality, and this is a characteristic signature of chaotic systems. In fact, the attractor dimension is an invariant quantity for a given chaotic system, which means that it is unaffected by scaling, rotation, etc. The correlation dimension algorithm is normally used to estimate the dimension of a chaotic attractor from a time series. One first computes the correlation sum

$$C(\varepsilon) = \frac{2}{N(N-1)} \sum_{i=1}^{N} \sum_{j=i+1}^{N} \Theta(\varepsilon - \|x_i - x_j\|) \qquad (3.20)$$

where $N$ is the number of delay vectors, $\varepsilon$ is a neighborhood, $\Theta$ is the Heaviside step function, and $x_i$, $x_j$ are delay vectors. The sum simply counts the number of pairs of delay vectors that are within an $\varepsilon$-neighborhood of each other. For small values of $\varepsilon$ and infinite $N$, $C(\varepsilon) \propto \varepsilon^D$, and the correlation dimension $D$ is defined as

$$D = \lim_{\varepsilon \to 0} \lim_{N \to \infty} \frac{\partial \ln C(\varepsilon)}{\partial \ln \varepsilon} \qquad (3.21)$$

This dimension will yield the correct, integer values for nonfractal objects and is accepted as the best way of estimating a fractal attractor dimension from time series data. In order to use this algorithm for the practical analysis of a finite time series, the local slopes of the correlation sum are plotted against the neighborhood $\varepsilon$ on a semi-logarithmic scale for several embedding dimensions. If for all embedding dimensions $m > m_0$ there is a region where the curves all plateau and saturate at a single value, then that value is the correlation dimension. Note that the correlation sum can be computed automatically, while the correlation dimension has to be determined through expert interpretation [130].

### 3.3.2 Software Reliability Data

The analysis in this chapter involves three time series, each of which consists of interfailure times from a commercial software system. Each element of the time series is the time elapsed between the current failure and the last failure. The data are time-ordered, i.e. the interfailure times are recorded in the order in which they actually occurred, rather than being sorted into ascending order (as is often done in statistical reliability growth modeling). The noise known to be present in these datasets is discretization noise; the data are discretized to integer values, representing some time scale. For one time series, this time scale is the nearest second; for the other two time series, this time scale is the nearest *day*.

The first time series was collected by Musa [45]. It is referred to as "System 5," and consists of 831 interfailure times, recorded to the nearest second. The system from which this data was collected was a real-time commercial system, comprised of over 2.4 million object code instructions. The data set was collected during the system test phase of development, under careful controls. As with all datasets archived at this site, the data were collected during the 1970s. This particular dataset is the largest of the 16 software reliability datasets archived at [45].

The second time series was collected by IBM in the course of the Orthogonal Defect Classification (ODC) project. The dataset is archived in [174]. It consists of 1207 bug reports, each of which includes the date of the failure. Thus, this data is discretized only to the nearest day and is not presented as interfailure times. In order to convert this dataset to interfailure times, the recommendation in [174] to assume that failures arrive at random times during a day was followed. A uniform random number generator was used to determine the $j$-th interfailure time during a day, and then the total interfailure times during a day were normalized so they sum to 1.0. This technique is strikingly similar to a recommendation in [130]: discretization noise can be removed by first adding uniform white noise in the interval $[-0.5, 0.5]$ to a signal, and then applying a nonlinear noise reduction scheme. This dataset will be referred to as "ODC1." The third dataset also comes from the IBM Orthogonal Defect Classification project, and is also archived in [174]. This dataset consists of 2008 bug reports, with the date of each report attached, as in ODC1. Preprocessing of this dataset was conducted in the same manner as for ODC1. We will refer to this dataset as "ODC4."

## 3.4 Experimental Results

The experiments reported in this section follow the procedures described in Section 3.3. First, the state-space reconstruction of each system is described, along with the evidence that the time series arise from a stationary process. Next, the surrogate data experiment is presented; the resulting evidence of deterministic behavior is the main result of this chapter. Finally, the evidence obtained for chaotic behavior is discussed.

### 3.4.1 State Space Reconstruction

The first problem was to reconstruct the state space for each of the three datasets. The method of delay embeddings described in Section 3 was used; this requires determining values for the time lag $v$ and the embedding dimension $m$. The mutual information statistic and the autocorrelation function were computed for values of $v$ between one and six for System 5, and between one and four for ODC1 and ODC4. Those results are presented in Table 1. The first minimum of the mutual information statistic occurred at $v \leq 4$ for each dataset, but there were no zero crossings for the autocorrelation function in that range. The two-dimensional phase portraits for each system were then examined for delays $v = 1$-6. Delays of $v = 4$, $v = 3$, and $v = 5$ resulted in the largest apparent structures for System 5, ODC1 and ODC4, respectively. Those "best" phase portraits are shown in Figures 3.7-3.9, respectively (these figures may be found at the end of the chapter).

Qualitatively, the phase portraits for each dataset appear to show the following characteristics: firstly, in the System 5 phase portrait, structures on the order of $10^4$ units in size appear; these structures are apparent trajectories and voids in the phase plane. In the ODC1 phase portraits, some structure appears on the order of 0.3 units in size; this is less than the expected noise amplitude, so these structures are not very significant. Finally, in ODC4, a dramatic structure (a *double helix*) shows up along the $y$-axis. It is 4 units in length, well above the noise level. Taking these three phase portraits together, the datasets seem to show some indications of deterministic behavior. The next step is to estimate the dimensionality of each state space, and to determine if the datasets are stationary.

Table 3.1: Mutual Information and Autocorrelation Values

|  | $v = 1$ | $v = 2$ | $v = 3$ | $v = 4$ | $v = 5$ | $v = 6$ |
|---|---|---|---|---|---|---|
| System-5 Mutual Inf. | 0.077 | 0.082 | 0.089 | 0.067 | 0.082 | 0.070 |
| System-5 Autocorrelation | 0.138 | 0.152 | 0.126 | 0.087 | 0.119 | 0.114 |
| ODC1 Mutual Inf. | 0.036 | 0.011 | 0.072 | 0.041 | - | - |
| ODC1 Autocorrelation | 0.328 | 0.101 | 0.070 | 0.043 | - | - |
| ODC4 Mutual Inf. | 0.021 | 0.012 | 0.020 | 0.015 | - | - |
| ODC4 Autocorrelation | 0.229 | 0.167 | 0.174 | 0.124 | - | - |

Using the technique of false nearest neighbors yields the results given in Figure 3.10. For each dataset, the goal is a value of $m$ such that the ratio of false nearest neighbors drops to 0. Both System 5 and ODC1 reach this point by $m = 8$; to be conservative, a value of $m = 9$ is used for the experiments in this section. ODC4 is a more difficult case, since the ratio of false nearest neighbors becomes very small, but never actually reaches 0; in fact, one can see the beginning of an oscillation by $m = 16$. In the remainder of this paper, a value of $m = 15$ will be used for ODC4, since this is the largest value of *m* before the oscillatory behavior begins. To summarize, System 5 is reconstructed in 9 dimensions with a delay of 4, ODC1 in 9 dimensions with a delay of 3, and ODC4 in 15 dimensions with a delay of 5.

Space-time separation plots for System 5, ODC1, and ODC4 are shown in Figures 3.11, 3.12, and 3.13, respectively. All three datasets appear to be stationary, since the curves in each plot saturate at a rough plateau. Temporal correlations in estimating the attractor dimension can be avoided if points closer than 50 time steps together in System 5, closer than 35 time steps in ODC1, and closer than 70 time steps in ODC4 are excluded when computing the correlation sum.

### 3.4.2 Test for Determinism

One of the key steps in nonlinear time series analysis is ensuring that one does not try to estimate chaotic invariants for a linear stochastic process. While in theory a white-noise process is infinite-dimensional, low dimensional values can often be obtained for finite times series consisting of white noise. The correlation dimension algorithm, along with other estimators for chaotic invariants, quantifies deterministic behaviors *when they are known to be present*. These algorithms are not effective as tests for determinism in and of themselves. The method of surrogate data [283] was developed to provide scientific evidence that a time series does in fact exhibit deterministic, rather than random, behavior. This technique is based on statistical hypothesis testing; the null hypothesis is that the time series arises from a linear stochastic process, and the alternative is that the time series arises from a deterministic process.

The method of surrogate data was used to test each of the three datasets for the presence of deterministic behavior. First, 22 analytic probability distributions were fitted to each dataset, including the normal, lognormal, 2-parameter Weibull, 2-paramter Gamma, exponential, Rayleigh and Beta distributions. The Kolomogorov-Smirnoff goodness-of-fit test was then used to determine if any of the distributions were a good match for the datasets. At a significance of 0.05, the test rejects every distribution for each dataset. Thus, no probability structure for the datasets has been found. Therefore, in these experiments, the null hypothesis of a linear Gaussian process, distorted by a monotonic, invertible nonlinear observation (the most general hypothesis available in the literature) was used, with a significance of 0.05. Thus, 39 surrogates were generated for each dataset, and the null hypothesis was rejected if the statistic value for the original time series was greater or less than all the surrogates. The results of these experiments are summarized in Table 2, where the statistic values for the original dataset, along with the minimum, and maximum of the surrogate values, are presented.

Table 3.2: Test Statistics

| | *Original* | *Surrogate Minimum* | *Surrogate Maximum* |
|---|---|---|---|
| System 5 Time Reversal | 3097.5 | −24794.4 | 20981.7 |
| System 5 Prediction | 39053.1 | 37412.7734 | 39049.5 |
| ODC1 Time Reversal | −1.31 | −0.36 | 0.26 |
| ODC4 Time Reversal | −2.85 | −6.56 | 4.97 |
| ODC4 Prediction | 0.84 | 1.17 | 1.82 |

Examining Table 2, the null hypothesis is rejected on dataset ODC1 using time reversal, but accepted for System 5 and ODC4 using time reversal. The null hypothesis is rejected for both System 5 and ODC4 using the more powerful prediction error statistic [130]. Table 2, taken together with the earlier attempt to fit a classical distribution to the datasets, provides quantitative evidence that these datasets are deterministic in nature. This means that the stochastic models usually used in software reliability modeling do not capture the full state of nature in software reliability growth; deterministic dynamics appear to be present and (at least in the case of the three datasets we have analyzed) to dominate any random behaviors. This analysis implies that deterministic models (such as neural networks) would be a better fit for software reliability data, and could provide better predictions of reliability growth and when to stop testing than stochastic models. This is the principal result of this chapter; attempts to find a correlation dimension for each dataset are discussed in the next section.

### *3.4.3 Dimensions*

One of the characteristics of a chaotic system is that the attractor in phase space has a fractal geometry [130]. This means the attractor is self-similar over some range of length scales, and has a noninteger dimensionality. An attempt was made to determine if the phase-space attractors for the datasets under study are in fact fractal objects, using the correlation dimension algorithm. First, an estimate of the fractal dimension was made for the raw datasets; the scaling plots for System 5, ODC1 and ODC4 are given in Figures 3.14, 3.15 and 3.16, respectively. Notice that System 5 shows a common behavior and a small plateau right around $10^4$. However, the curves do not converge to a single value, but differ by a factor. For this dataset, the evidence of fractal behavior is suggestive, but not definitive. The plot for ODC1, while having a roughly similar shape, is considerably weaker. Some common behavior is present, but there is really not a clear plateau, nor do the curves converge. The plot for ODC4 does not seem to show fractal behavior. Next, the locally constant nonlinear noise reduction scheme [130] was used to filter the datasets. Scaling plots for the filtered versions of System 5, ODC1, and ODC4 are shown in Figures 3.17, 3.18 and 3.19, respectively. The filtered time series actually appear to show *less* evidence of fractal behavior. These analyses indicate that there is some behavior in one dataset that is suggestive of chaotic dynamics, but this evidence is too weak to support a definitive conclusion concerning the presence of chaotic behavior in software reliability growth data.

### 3.5 Remarks

We expect software reliability to be the key technological bottleneck of the 21$^{st}$ century. Software engineers and researchers do not have a full understanding of the reliability growth process in software, while software systems are too complex. The stochastic failure models used to date apparently do not match the characteristics of software failures, as they cannot account for the deterministic dynamics we have detected in our datasets. The research reported in this chapter represents a first step in applying the techniques of fractal sets and chaos theory to this problem. We have suggested a causal model for software failures, in which the fault set of a program is hypothesized to be a fractal subset of the input space for that program. An implication of this hypothesis is that a software reliability growth dataset will show deterministic, and possibly chaotic, behavior as opposed to stochastic behavior. A statistical experiment demonstrates deterministic behavior in three software reliability growth datasets, and suggestive but not definitive evidence of chaotic behavior was found in one of those datasets. Further research in this area, including the use of deterministic models for predicting software reliability growth, may be found in [310].

Software reliability growth models are one tool used by developers to estimate the quality of a software system. These models, however, can only be applied late in the development cycle, when testing and failure data become available. The problem is that this is also the most expensive part of the development cycle to find software faults; eliminating faults earlier on in development is highly desirable. Hence, early in the development cycle, software engineers try to determine which software modules pose a high risk of failure. These modules are then treated as major risks in the development effort, and additional resources are directed towards their development and testing. The primary tools used in deciding which modules are development risks are software metrics, which represent a different mechanism for summarizing the characteristics of a program. The next two chapters of this book will examine the usage of machine learning and data mining technologies for the analysis of software metrics.

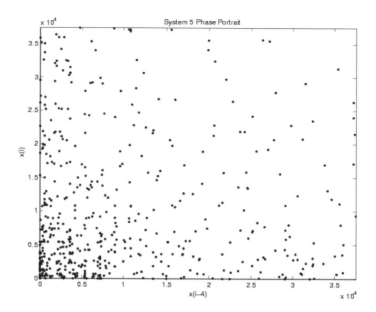

Figure 3.7: System 5 Phase Portrait, $v = 4$

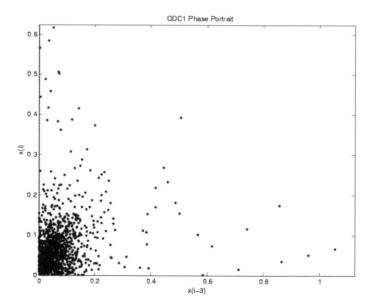

Figure 3.8: ODC1 Phase Portrait, $v = 3$

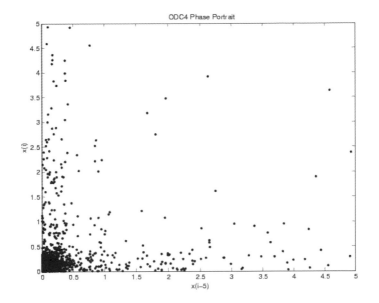

Figure 3.9: ODC4 Phase Portrait, $v = 5$

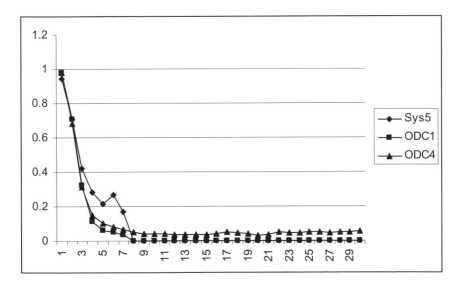

Figure 3.10: False Nearest Neighbor Ratios

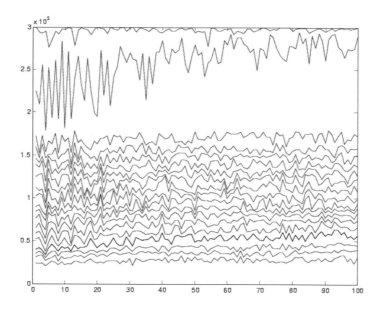

Figure 3.11: Space-Time Separation Plot for System 5

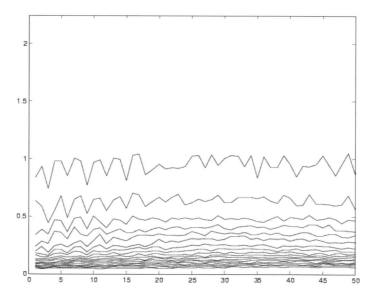

Figure 3.12: Space-Time Separation Plot for ODC1

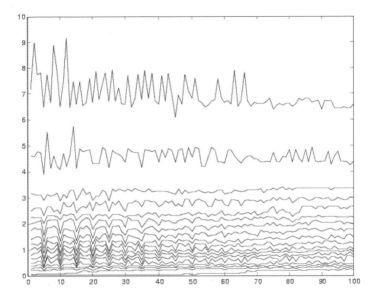

Figure 3.13: Space-Time Separation plot for ODC4

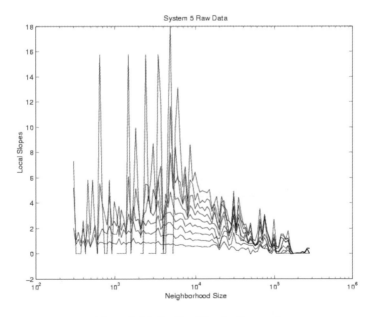

Figure 3.14: Scaling Plot for System 5

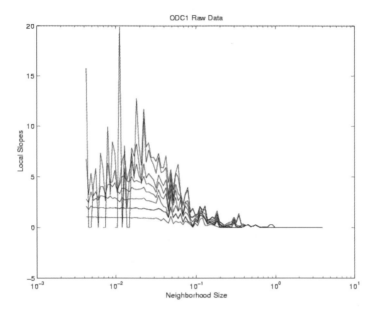

Figure 3.15: Scaling Plot for ODC1

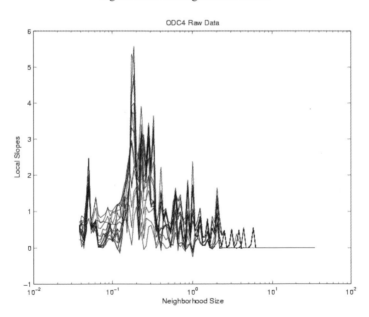

Figure 3.16: Scaling Plot for ODC4

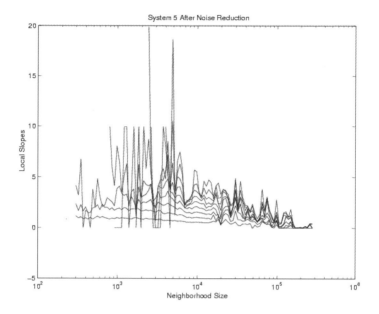

Figure 3.17: Scaling Plot for System 5, After Noise Reduction

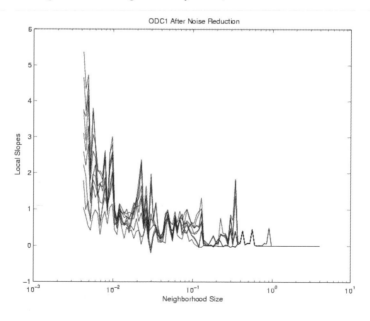

Figure 3.18: Scaling Plot for ODC1, After Noise Reduction

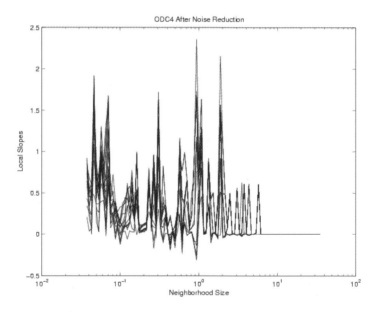

Figure 3.19: Scaling Plot for ODC4, After Noise Reduction

# Chapter 4

# Data Mining and Software Metrics

## 4.1 Introduction

Machine learning and data mining are powerful techniques for discovering inherent relationships within a collection of data. Machine learning algorithms will generally focus on creating an internal representation of a problem domain for the use of a machine (such as the connection weights in a neural network), while data mining algorithms usually generate models principally for human interpretation. There have been a number of works reported on the application of machine learning and data mining techniques to the problem of software quality [47, 67, 68, 93, 95, 133, 138, 139, 140, 143, 266]. The majority of these papers use software metrics as predictor attributes, and observed failures or changes as the dependent attribute. The majority also employ some form of supervised learning, be it statistical regression, neural networks, genetic algorithms, or others. Very few unsupervised learning algorithms have been used in the software quality domain. In fact, fuzzy c-means clustering has not been used in this domain at all!

This chapter describes new research in the use of machine learning and data mining techniques in the software quality domain. This work revolves around the use of fuzzy clustering and freely available data mining tools for the analysis of software metric databases. A few other authors have also investigated the use of data mining of software metrics. A call for the use of data mining to assist in the management of software projects is made in [226], and some candidate techniques are discussed, including multiple regression analysis, Principal Components Analysis, neural networks and classification trees. Mendonca et al. [188] utilize a combination of artificial intelligence techniques and statistical analysis to mine software metrics. The AI technique used is called the Goal-Question-Metric technique, and is a mechanism for generating queries based on user goals and identifying metrics that can provide a useful answer to these questions. The statistical tools employed are correlation analyses and a search for outliers in a database. A validation of this approach, principally using data user surveys, is reported in [189]. McLellan et al. report on data mining efforts carried out in a reusable component library at Schlumberger Oilfield Services [184]. They use the terms *software mining* and *shotgun approach* to describe a large exploratory data mining project. What is unique about their algorithms is that the data to be analyzed is raw source code, rather than a table of metric values. The analysis tools are custom-built awk scripts, which are used to crawl the library and extract metric values. The extracted values are then imported to an Oracle database. While the analysis in that paper does not extend beyond basic statistics of the resulting tables, the potential for using more advanced techniques is obvious. Khoshgoftaar et al. [139] report on the use of knowledge discovery in databases (KDD) for predicting software quality from software metrics. They studied a large telecommunications software system, and its associated configuration management and problem reporting databases. The system's modules were divided into two classes: those that had experienced a failure during customer operation, and those that had not. The data mining tool used was the Classification and Regression Tree (CART) algorithm. A tenfold cross-validation experiment with this tool obtained an average testing classification accuracy of around 75%. Shin and Goel [266] utilized a radial basis function network instead of the CART algorithm for data mining in a NASA database of software metrics. A bootstrap technique was used to validate the classification results.

The investigation reported in this chapter looks at software metrics from the point of view of granular computing (see Chapter 1). The goal is to conduct a granular analysis of the datasets, instead of finding a regression model to relate metrics and module changes. Fuzzy clustering in metrics datasets that are *not* associated with a failure count, which is the situation developers face early in the software development cycle, are also explored. Failure counts are not always available, especially in the early stages of software development. This is a significant problem, since the data mining and machine learning algorithms utilized to date almost exclusively rely on *supervised learning*, a form of machine learning which requires both a set of feature vectors to analyze, *and* the true classification of those feature vectors. Without failure counts, these algorithms quite literally have nothing to learn from. *Unsupervised learning*, on the other hand, searches for knowledge within a dataset *without* needing to be told the true classification of a feature vector. Thus, unsupervised learning algorithms can be used before any failures have been observed. When failure counts *are* available, unsupervised learning can also help identify the knowledge present in the feature vectors, and relate that knowledge to the observed failures. This investigation illustrates how both tasks may be approached; however, the primary goal is cluster analysis, not model-building [306, 307, 308].

The remainder of this chapter is organized as follows. In Section 2, machine learning and data mining for software quality are reviewed. In Section 3, the datasets under study are characterized, and previous work involving those datasets reviewed. Section 4 describes the fuzzy clustering experiments on the datasets, and section 5 presents the results of using the Info-Fuzzy Network and tools from WizSoft® on these data sets.

## 4.2 Review of Related Work

In this Section, the relevant literature from machine learning and data mining is discussed. The focus of this review is on the use of machine learning in the software quality domain, fuzzy cluster analysis, and feature reduction.

### 4.2.1 Machine Learning for Software Quality

As described in Chapters 1 and 2, the effort to improve software quality is a multi-faceted, ongoing area of research. A few companies, such as IBM or AT&T are reasonably good at building large, high-quality applications, but they are the exceptions. For most organizations, large size and high quality are almost mutually exclusive [121, 122]. The majority of software quality initiatives collect software metrics and attempt to use this data for software process control. Statistical methods are predominately used for these analyses, even though software metrics are very poor candidates for statistical analysis. Different metrics tend to be highly correlated, and the data collected from any project or group of projects tends to be skewed towards small modules with low failure rates.

Not surprisingly, soft computing techniques for modeling software metrics have also been tried. Neural networks [93, 133, 138, 143, 266], neuro-fuzzy systems [7, 190], fuzzy logic and classification [67, 68, 95], genetic programming [141], genetic-fuzzy systems [8], and classification trees [47, 139, 140], have been tried on various datasets. Multilayer perceptrons, in particular, are one of the more popular non-parametric techniques used in the analysis of software metric data. As mentioned, a constant problem for both statistical and soft computing approaches is that the data are heavily skewed in favor of modules with relatively few failures and relatively low metric values. This can be an especially serious problem for machine learning approaches that try to optimize a global measure of predictive accuracy; "always guessing the majority class" is a common mistake for learning algorithms in such skewed datasets. In [139], this issue of skewness was accounted for by the use of differing misclassification penalties. A greater cost was associated with classifying high-risk modules as low risk than with classifying low risk modules as high risk. While this approach can improve the learning process in a skewed dataset, the results are highly sensitive to the ratio between the different misclassification penalties. We will describe experiments using an alternative technique for homogenizing class distributions, known as resampling, in Chapter 5.

Our investigation utilizes fuzzy c-means clustering, and is the first to do so in this domain. The only other use of fuzzy clustering is a fuzzy subtractive clustering approach used in [304]. The fuzzy subtractive clustering algorithm requires that expected cluster characteristics be specified *a priori*, and so is not very useful as an exploratory tool. The power of a clustering algorithm is that it does not rely on predefined "classes" in the way that neural networks and other supervised learning approaches do. Instead, clustering algorithms search for the structures naturally present in the data. Failure classes can be generated by treating each cluster as a class. If the clustering algorithm is itself fuzzy, then the resulting classes are fuzzy, and have imprecise boundaries. This is a better representation of the true state of nature in software failure analysis [8, 47].

### 4.2.2 Fuzzy Cluster Analysis

Traditionally, cluster analysis has utilized classical set theory. An object is either a member of one particular subset, or it is *not* a member of that subset. Furthermore, each subset must be disjoint, and they must together form a partition of the total set of objects. This approach, while mathematically sound, cannot account for the ambiguity and noise that always accompany real-world objects. Fuzzy cluster analysis was developed to permit some ambiguity and noise in a robust clustering algorithm. A fuzzy cluster is a set to which an object may *partly* belong, to a degree indicated by the *membership* value for that point in that cluster. A *fuzzy partition* is a partition in which an object may belong to several subsets, so long as the sum of that object's membership values

$$\sum_i \mu_i = 1 \quad [110].$$

The most common clustering algorithm underlying fuzzy cluster analysis is the well-known Fuzzy c-Means (FCM) algorithm [110]. This is an iterative algorithm that attempts to find clusters that minimize the cost function

$$J(f) = \sum_{x \in X} \sum_{k \in K} f^m(x)(k) \cdot d^2(x, k) \tag{4.1}$$

where $f$ is a fuzzy partition, $f(x)(k)$ is the membership of pattern $x$ in cluster $k$, $m$ is the *fuzzifier* exponent, and $d(x,k)$ is the distance between pattern $x$ and the prototype (centroid) of the $k$-th cluster. FCM is an iterative optimization algorithm, in which the optimization of cluster prototypes and the optimization of cluster memberships alternate. FCM requires a set of patterns (represented as vectors), a distance metric (usually the Euclidean distance), and the expected number of clusters in the set of patterns. The initial set of cluster prototypes is chosen randomly, and the fuzzy partition $f$ is computed for these cluster centers. Then in each subsequent stage, the cluster prototypes are changed to optimize $J$ with $f$ held constant, and then $f$ is changed to optimize $J$ with the cluster prototypes held constant. The algorithm terminates when the improvement of $J$ from the previous iteration falls below a minimum threshold, or a maximum number of iterations is exceeded.

FCM is an unsupervised learning scheme. In general, the patterns that are to be clustered do not include class or value information. It is the distribution of patterns in feature space that determines which patterns will be assigned to a cluster. FCM optimizes $J$ for a given set of patterns and a given number of clusters. However, FCM provides no guidance on what the correct number of clusters *is*. Finding the correct number of clusters is known as the *cluster validity problem*, and there is no general theory on how to solve it. What is normally done is to run the FCM algorithm on a dataset several times, using different numbers of clusters. Then, measures of the "quality" of the resulting fuzzy partitions are taken by computing *cluster validity metrics* for each fuzzy partition. The partition with the optimum value for these cluster validity metrics is considered correct [110].

The final value of the objective function $J$ is monotonic decreasing with respect to the number of clusters $c$, and so is not useful as a criterion for deciding the correct value of $c$ [110]. Instead, measures such as the partition coefficient [18], proportion exponent [297], separation index [64], and a fuzzy separation index [300] are used. These measures are all based on some notion of what a generically "good" partition would look like. Compactness and separation of clusters is one criterion; minimal ambiguity (i.e. the values of $f(x)(k)$ approach 1 or 0) is another. There is currently no way to determine *a priori* which of these metrics will be most appropriate for a given dataset. If the class labels or output values for the dataset happen to be available, a customized cluster validity metric based on that information is generally the best choice, as this information establishes the true (state-of-nature) mapping between features and classes [110].

### *4.2.3 Feature Space Reduction*

It is often possible to express the same information that exists in a dataset using fewer attributes. Doing so can reduce the computational burden of automatic pattern recognition or classification. In addition, feature reduction can also remove noise from a dataset, and thus improve the performance of a clustering algorithm. One of the most common approaches in this area is Principal Components Analysis (PCA). PCA is based on the notion that points in the dataset form a hyperellipsoid in feature space, and that this hyperellipsoid has a few large axes and many small ones. PCA determines the directions of the axes of this hyperellipsoid and the length of these axes. For feature vectors with $n$ components, form the $n \times n$ covariance matrix $\Sigma$ for the data set. This matrix records the covariance between the $i$-th and $j$-th attributes, $i, j \in \{1, 2, ..., n\}$ as $\Sigma(i,j)$. Then the eigenvectors and eigenvalues of $\Sigma$ are determined. Normally, one finds a few large eigenvalues and several smaller eigenvalues. The large eigenvalues indicate axes of the hyperellipsoid that carry a significant amount of information about the dataset; smaller eigenvalues are assumed to represent noise dimensions. The axes themselves are defined by the eigenvectors associated with each eigenvalue. Feature reduction is carried out by forming a matrix $A$ of the significant eigenvectors, and then applying the transformation

$$\vec{y} = A^{t}(\vec{x} - \vec{\mu}) \qquad (4.2)$$

to every feature vector x, where $\mu$ is the mean vector of the dataset. The resulting dataset will have as many attributes as there were significant eigenvectors, will be oriented in parallel with the axes of the hyperellipsoid, and will have its origin at the mean point of the dataset. Furthermore, each axis of the hyperellipsoid is orthogonal to every other axis, implying statistical independence. Other techniques of feature reduction include Nonlinear Component Analysis and Independent Component Analysis, to name a few [59].

## 4.3 Software Change and Software Characteristic Datasets

The datasets examined in this study were generated in the course of two Master's theses at the University of Wisconsin-Milwaukee. The MIS dataset was collected by Randy Lind in [166] and widely disseminated in [175], while the datasets we have labeled "OOSoft" "ProcSoft" were Collected by Warren DeVilbiss in [52]. In this section, a detailed description of the datasets is provided, and the results of previous work on these datasets examined.

### *4.3.1 The MIS Dataset*

This dataset consists of 390 records, each having 12 fields. The first 11 fields are the values of different software metrics for a module, and the final field is the number of changes made to that module. Lind assumed that the number of changes in a module corresponds to the number of failures in that module [166]. The application that was analyzed is a commercial medical imaging system, General Electric's SIGNA system, running on a Data General MV4000 computer. In total, the system is comprised of approximately 400,000 lines of source code, divided into 4500 modules. Of these modules, 58% were written in Pascal, 29% were written in Fortran, 7% in assembly language, and 6% in PL/M (the Intel-86 programming language for microcomputers). The dataset itself was created by extracting the software metrics for a sample of 390 modules written in Fortran and Pascal, and associating those values with the number of changes that had to be made for each module [166]. The metrics used in this data set are as follows:

    i.     The number of lines of source code
    ii.    The number of executable lines (rather than comments or whitespace)
   iii.   The total number of characters
   iv.   The number of comment lines
    v.    The number of comment characters
   vi.   The number of code characters
  vii.   Halstead's N – defined as the number of operators plus the number of operands [97]

viii.    Halstead's $N^{\wedge}$ – an approximation to N [97]
ix.    Jensen's NF – another approximation to N [118]
x.    McCabe's cyclomatic complexity [181]
xi.    Bandwidth [232]

An important point about this dataset is what constitutes a "module." Non-integer values like "8.5" were reported in this dataset for McCabe's cyclomatic complexity – a metric which should always consist of integer values. While this point is not specifically addressed in [166], it turns out that a "module" in this dataset is a source file, which may contain one or more routines. The value of the counting metrics, such as the lines of source code or the number of comment characters, has been determined by summing the values over all routines in a module. The values of the complexity metrics, such as Bandwidth or McCabe's cyclomatic complexity, have been determined by *averaging* over all routines in a module. Thus, the granularity of this dataset is fairly coarse. (As a side note, McCabe's original paper does account for modules composed of individual functions. The rule typically used to determine cyclomatic complexity, "number of decisions + 1," is actually the special case where cyclomatic complexity is determined for a single function. In [181], multiple functions are each treated as a strongly-connected component, and the total complexity is the sum of their individual complexities. Thus, in a module with multiple functions, it is actually better to sum the cyclomatic complexity values, rather than averaging them.)

Lind's thesis reports on the result of a linear correlation analysis of this dataset. Pearson's correlation coefficient is computed between each metric and the change count. For the reader's convenience, we reproduce these results in Table 4.1. Notice that there is generally a strong positive correlation between each metric and the number of changes, except for Bandwidth.

In addition to [166], Lind and Vairavan published a paper summarizing these results [167]. Another work that examines the MIS dataset is [205], in which the authors apply Principal Components Analysis as well. In this work, the number of principal dimensions was found to be two, rather than one as reported later in this chapter. The difference is that in [205], the PCA algorithm was applied to the raw dataset, whereas the dataset was normalized first in the current investigation. Normalization is an important step, because differences in scale across different dimensions can distort the distribution of a multi-dimensional database. The PCA algorithm assumes a hyperellipsoidal distribution of data; distortions introduced by axis scalings can distort the true distribution, altering the orientation and size of the different axes.

Table 4.1: Correlation of Metrics to Changes, from [166]

| Metric | Correlation to Changes |
|---|---|
| Total Lines | 0.73 |
| Code Lines | 0.68 |
| Total Chars | 0.72 |
| Comments | 0.75 |
| Comment Chars | 0.66 |
| Code Chars | 0.69 |
| Halstead's N | 0.62 |
| Halstead's N^ | 0.66 |
| Jensen's NF | 0.66 |
| McCabe's | 0.68 |
| Bandwidth | 0.26 |

Another work that examines this dataset is [133]. In this paper, the authors use neural networks for software reliability prediction and to identify fault-prone modules. The MIS dataset is used to illustrate the second objective. The 390 records are first classified into low-, medium-, and high-risk modules. The criterion used is that a low-risk module had no faults or one fault, medium-risk modules had two to nine faults, and high-risk modules had 10 or more faults. The study considers only the 203 low- and high- risk modules; the medium-risk modules were discarded. The network was then trained to distinguish between low-risk and high-risk modules.

There are two important points to notice about [133]. Firstly, the "hard" classification of modules based on the number of changes is a poor and arbitrary choice. No analysis has been conducted that showed that a module with nine changes was substantially different than one with 10 changes. This artificial classification can dramatically *worsen* the performance of a neural network classifier. This is because the underlying assumption of a neural network is that the input/output pairings it is trained on represent *actual observations*, not subjective judgments. The network will *always* seek a smooth mapping from inputs to outputs, even when the introduction of subjective judgments has destroyed the actual mapping. Second, results in the current investigation show that the fault classes that exist in the MIS dataset are in fact overlapping, *fuzzy* classes. The artificial imposition of hard boundaries, which are not truly representative of the data, will also distort a neural network classifier's results.

### 4.3.2 The OOSoft and ProcSoft Datasets

The two remaining datasets contain records of software metrics that are not associated with a change count, drawn from [52]. Both datasets are from operator display applications, which allow limited data entry. These datasets are designated as ProcSoft and OOSoft. The application underlying the ProcSoft dataset was programmed using structured analysis techniques, in a mixture of C and assembly language. The assembly language code was primarily for device drivers, and was ignored in that thesis. The application underlying OOSoft was developed using object-oriented techniques. This program incorporates additional functionality over and above the functionality of the first program. In order to make a comparison, 422 functions from the first program were analyzed, and 562 methods from the object-oriented program performing the same functionality were analyzed. Functions from the structured program, and methods from the object-oriented program, were treated as the basic modules of the program. Thus, these datasets represent a more fine-grained analysis than the MIS dataset.

The OOSoft dataset contains 562 records, and the ProcSoft dataset contains 422 records, with each record representing one method or function. There were a total of 11 measures computed for each function or method. These are:

 i.  n1 – The number of unique operators
 ii.  n2 – The number of unique operands

iii.    N1 – The number of operators
iv.    N2 – The number of operands
v.    Halstead's N [97]
vi.    Halstead's N^ [97]
vii.    Jensen's NF [118]
viii.    VG1 – McCabe's cyclomatic complexity [181]
ix.    VG2 – McCabe's cyclomatic complexity, enhanced to include the number of predicates in decisions [52]
x.    Lines of Code (LOC)
xi.    Lines of Comments (CMT)

DeVilbiss examined the linear correlations between each pair of metrics in each dataset – excluding N, N^, and NF – again using Pearson's correlation coefficient. For the reader's convenience, those results are reproduced in Tables 4.2 & 4.3 below.

Table 4.2: Pairwise Correlations in ProcSoft, from [52]

|       | *n1* | *n2*  | *N1*  | *N2*  | *VG1* | *VG2* | *LOC* | *CMT* |
|-------|------|-------|-------|-------|-------|-------|-------|-------|
| n1    | 1.0  | 0.837 | 0.817 | 0.791 | 0.771 | 0.785 | 0.751 | 0.553 |
| n2    |      | 1.0   | 0.933 | 0.948 | 0.864 | 0.857 | 0.806 | 0.554 |
| N1    |      |       | 1.0   | 0.984 | 0.912 | 0.914 | 0.829 | 0.534 |
| N2    |      |       |       | 1.0   | 0.879 | 0.877 | 0.820 | 0.531 |
| VG1   |      |       |       |       | 1.0   | 0.982 | 0.760 | 0.476 |
| VG2   |      |       |       |       |       | 1.0   | 0.755 | 0.475 |
| LOC   |      |       |       |       |       |       | 1.0   | 0.908 |
| CMT   |      |       |       |       |       |       |       | 1.0   |

Table 4.3: Pairwise Correlations in OOSoft, from [52]

|       | *n1* | *n2*  | *N1*  | *N2*  | *VG1* | *VG2* | *LOC* | *CMT*  |
|-------|------|-------|-------|-------|-------|-------|-------|--------|
| n1    | 1.0  | 0.814 | 0.796 | 0.681 | 0.636 | 0.597 | 0.193 | -0.107 |
| n2    |      | 1.0   | 0.869 | 0.883 | 0.678 | 0.670 | 0.318 | -0.010 |
| N1    |      |       | 1.0   | 0.952 | 0.882 | 0.864 | 0.447 | 0.072  |
| N2    |      |       |       | 1.0   | 0.804 | 0.817 | 0.472 | 0.113  |
| VG1   |      |       |       |       | 1.0   | 0.961 | 0.484 | 0.148  |
| VG2   |      |       |       |       |       | 1.0   | 0.472 | 0.147  |
| LOC   |      |       |       |       |       |       | 1.0   | 0.92   |
| CMT   |      |       |       |       |       |       |       | 1.0    |

Note that in Table 4.2, all the metrics correlated well with each other, with the exception of the number of lines of comments. In Table 4.3, the correlation values tended to be lower. In that dataset, DeVilbiss identified a trend of similar metrics (such as the various metrics due to Halstead [97]) being more correlated to each other than to different "families" of metrics. Also, the number of lines of code and of comments correlated well only with each other. ProcSoft and OOSoft will be an important part of the analysis in this chapter, because they represent the reality of software development: software developers will simply not have access to change data until late in the development cycle, and so must work with metric values only.

## 4.4 Fuzzy Cluster Analysis

This section describes the methodology and results of a fuzzy cluster analysis on the MIS, OOSoft and ProcSoft datasets. The datasets contain no missing values, and all attribute values were normalized to [0,1]. The Fuzzy c-means algorithm in MATLAB® 6.0 was used in all experiments, with a fuzzifier value of 2 and a stopping criterion of minimal improvement of 0.00001. The number of clusters ranged from 2 to 10, and the cluster validity metrics used were the partition coefficient [18], the CS index [64], the Separation index [300], and (in the case of the MIS dataset) the average sum of squared error (SSE) in a ten-fold cross-validation experiment.

### 4.4.1 Results for the MIS Dataset

We allowed the number of clusters in this dataset to range from 2 to 10. Table 4.4 presents the values of the partition coefficient, CS index, and Separation index, as well as the average SSE of the tenfold cross-validation experiment, for each number of clusters. The SSE in a single partition is the testing SSE for one tenth of the dataset, after the dataset was clustered using the other nine tenths. The change value for each cluster was determined by taking the centroid of the change counts for that cluster, using

$$F_i = \frac{\sum_{x \in C_i} \mu_{ij}(x_j) f(x_j)}{\sum_{x \in C_i} \mu_{ij}(x_j)} \qquad (4.3)$$

where $F_i$ is the number of changes for the $i$-th cluster, $C_i$ is the $i$-th cluster, $x_j$ is the $j$-th record from the dataset, $f(x_j)$ is the change count for record $x$, and $\mu_{ij}$ is the membership of the $j$-th record in the $i$-th cluster. In the testing phase, the fuzzy nearest prototypes algorithm [135] was used to determine the inferred change value of a record. This algorithm takes a feature vector, and determines the fuzzy classification of that vector based on an existing fuzzy partition, which is exactly what is required for this step of the cluster analysis. The squared difference was taken between the inferred and actual value of the change count. Finally, the mean of the SSE values for all ten partitions was used as a cluster validity measure. Since this measure is specific to the dataset, and uses the actual output values to evaluate cluster validity, this is the measure we used to determine the actual number of clusters in this dataset.

Table 4.4: Cluster Validity Measures for MIS

| Clusters | Partition Coef | CS Index | Separation | Average SSE * $10^3$ |
|---|---|---|---|---|
| 2 | 0.8832 | 0.0064 | 9.5549 | 3.3596 |
| 3 | 0.7275 | 0.0001 | 20.7707 | 2.7435 |
| 4 | 0.6529 | 0.0003 | 20.8820 | 2.7124 |
| 5 | 0.6031 | 0.0000 | 16.5433 | 2.5807 |
| 6 | 0.5145 | 0.0005 | 29.1250 | 2.5836 |
| 7 | 0.4865 | 0.0006 | 23.9647 | 2.5753 |
| 8 | 0.4262 | 0.0001 | 41.6580 | 2.5878 |
| 9 | 0.4060 | 0.0001 | 40.0919 | 2.5762 |
| 10 | 0.4014 | 0.0009 | 26.0038 | 2.5821 |

Maximal values of the partition coefficient and the CS index indicate the best partition; minimal values of the Separation index and the average SSE indicate the best partition. Clearly, the three generic metrics indicate that two clusters is the best partitioning, while the average SSE indicates that seven clusters are best. Furthermore, an examination of Table 4.4 shows that the CS index and the Separation index also achieve local extrema at seven clusters. In Figure 1, the values of the CS index, Separation index and average SSE are plotted together to illustrate this point. Since the average SSE makes use of the true output values in assessing cluster validity, and since the CS and Separation indices provide some additional support for this value, seven clusters will be accepted as the correct value in the remainder of this investigation. Note that the average SSE index is also vulnerable to skewness, and the CS index is known to be very sensitive to outliers. It is therefore significant that these three metrics all provide support for a partition of seven clusters.

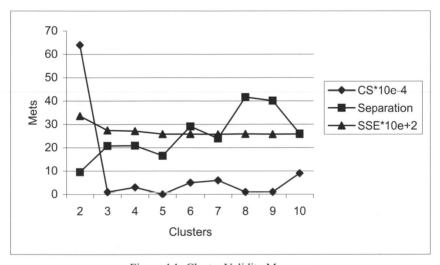

Figure 4.1: Cluster Validity Measures

Table 4.5 presents a statistical characterization of the change counts in the seven clusters identified as the best partition. The minimum, maximum, mean, median, and sample standard deviation of the changes per module, and the number of data elements present in each cluster after it was "hardened" using the maximum-membership method [110], are presented for each cluster. Also, the change value for each cluster centroid, as computed by Eq. (4.3) over the entire fuzzy cluster is included in Table 4.5. As the reader will note, there is extensive overlap between clusters in the change (output) dimension. This is evidence that changes are by nature fuzzy events; it is not possible to draw a clear line between high and low risk module classes based upon the number of changes. The reader will also note further evidence of skewness in this table. For each cluster, the median value of changes is substantially less than the mean, indicating the change distribution in the cluster is skewed towards a low occurrence of changes. Furthermore, the distribution of the data vectors is itself skewed towards clusters with low change counts. Finally, note that the clusters with the highest variance in the change counts are also the clusters with the highest mean values of the change counts, and the lowest number of data vectors.

Table 4.5: Cluster Characteristics in MIS

| Cluster | Min | Max | Mean | Median | STD | Count | Centroid |
|---------|-----|-----|------|--------|-----|-------|----------|
| 1 | 0 | 27 | 4.18 | 2 | 4.68 | 102 | 4.75 |
| 2 | 0 | 47 | 21.25 | 16.5 | 12.94 | 20 | 21.15 |
| 3 | 8 | 41 | 19.32 | 14 | 12.12 | 22 | 16.56 |
| 4 | 0 | 19 | 2.26 | 1 | 3.10 | 107 | 3.12 |
| 5 | 14 | 98 | 36.75 | 32.5 | 22.00 | 12 | 29.06 |
| 6 | 0 | 25 | 5.32 | 4 | 4.89 | 86 | 6.16 |
| 7 | 1 | 46 | 10.02 | 7 | 9.38 | 41 | 9.92 |

From a practical standpoint, this kind of cluster analysis will be most useful to software engineers as part of a Pareto analysis, in which modules are ranked according to increasing metric values. Ordinarily, the individual modules with the highest metric values are singled out for additional development effort. One alternative, supported by the current investigation, is to select modules belonging to the class or classes of modules that have high metric values for extra development work. This would capture a slightly different set of modules than a pure ranking scheme. The first step in performing such an analysis is to find a way to rank classes of modules. In the MIS dataset, the ordering of clusters based on individual metric values was examined. In Table 4.6, an ordering of clusters based on the cluster center component for a single metric is presented. The fact that all of the cluster centers, as well as the change centroids, have the same ordering indicates that a monotonic, granular relationship exists between metrics and changes. In particular, note the Bandwidth metric also obeys this relationship.

Table 4.6: Ordering of Cluster Centers by Attribute

| *Attribute* | *Ordering of Clusters* |
|---|---|
| Lines of Source Code | 4, 1, 6, 7, 3, 2, 5 |
| Executable Lines | 4, 1, 6, 7, 3, 2, 5 |
| Total Characters | 4, 1, 6, 7, 3, 2, 5 |
| Comment Lines | 4, 1, 6, 7, 3, 2, 5 |
| Comment Characters | 4, 1, 6, 7, 3, 2, 5 |
| Code Characters | 4, 1, 6, 7, 3, 2, 5 |
| Halstead's N | 4, 1, 6, 7, 3, 2, 5 |
| Halstead's N^ | 4, 1, 6, 7, 3, 2, 5 |
| Jensen's NF | 4, 1, 6, 7, 3, 2, 5 |
| McCabe's Cyclomatic Complexity | 4, 1, 6, 7, 3, 2, 5 |
| Bandwidth | 4, 1, 6, 7, 3, 2, 5 |
| **Change Centroids** | 4, 1, 6, 7, 3, 2, 5 |

We have used the Principal Components Analysis (PCA) algorithm to further characterize this dataset. The PCA algorithm assumes that feature vectors are distributed as a hyperellipsoid in feature space, and characterizes this hyperellipsoid. In using the PCA algorithm, one usually finds a few large eigenvalues, and then a number of small eigenvalues. Those large eigenvalues represent the important axes of the hyperellipsoid; the other dimensions are assumed to represent noise [59]. When the PCA algorithm was applied to the MIS dataset the largest eigenvalue was 0.2241, while the next-largest eigenvalue was 0.0139. Thus, this dataset has one principal dimension. Hence, MIS is a one-dimensional dataset, in which the clusters follow a monotonic relationship for all attributes. The overriding nature of this dataset is that it is monotonic for all attributes. Note that this is in contrast to the results reported in [166, 167], where Bandwidth was determined to have a low correlation. Correlation analysis is an important first step in data mining, but it is not the end of the story. A correlation coefficient expresses the degree to which two variables in a database are linearly dependent on each other. The correlation coefficient will *not* detect a strongly nonlinear relationship, nor can it detect linear relationships that are obscured by noise.   Thus, while a strong correlation is inherently meaningful as indicating a linear relationship, a low correlation does not rule out a linear relationship, and provides no information about whether a nonlinear relationship is at work.

Note also that these PCA results differ from those presented in [205], where the authors reported 2 principal dimensions. As noted earlier, attribute normalization was not carried out during that study. Furthermore, the two largest eigenvalues reported were 8.291 and 1.650. Note that the first eigenvalue is actually much larger than the second. The rule used to choose principal dimensions in [205] was to select those dimensions with eigenvalues $\geq 1$, rather than searching for the few "large" eigenvalues as recommended in the pattern recognition literature. The results presented in this investigation are thus consistent with the data in [205].

There is further evidence to show that  Bandwidth is an important metric. Another series of tenfold cross-validation experiments was performed on this dataset, allowing the number of clusters to vary between 2 and 16. In one of these experiments, all 11 metrics were used, including Bandwidth. In the other experiment, Bandwidth was dropped altogether. Table 4.7 shows the average SSE values per cluster for both experiments. As can be seen, removing Bandwidth decreases the predictive accuracy of the models for nearly every partition, with the lone exception being 11 clusters. 11 clusters is the optimum partition without Bandwidth; note that the average SSE is still higher than the optimum SSE with Bandwidth, which happens at seven clusters. Thus, Bandwidth is indeed an important metric (in contrast to the conclusions in [166, 167]), in the sense that it bears a similar relationship to the number of changes that other metrics do.

After reducing the dimensionality of the MIS dataset with the PCA algorithm, we re-ran our clustering experiment, to see how the clustering results change when noise is removed. Since the Fuzzy c-means algorithm requires at least two dimensions in a dataset, the eigenvectors corresponding to the two largest eigenvalues were used as features. As before, the values of the four clustering metrics for each partition from 2 to 16 clusters are reported in Table 4.8. The optimum partition, based on the average SSE metric, is nine clusters instead of seven. The other metrics do not seem to corroborate this value. There is only a local maximum in the CS index for this partition.

Table 4.7: Average SSE with and without Bandwidth

| Clusters | SSE $* 10^3$ with Band. | SSE $* 10^3$ without Band. |
|---|---|---|
| 2 | 3.3596 | 3.3703 |
| 3 | 2.7435 | 2.8428 |
| 4 | 2.7124 | 2.7697 |
| 5 | 2.5807 | 2.6404 |
| 6 | 2.5836 | 2.6267 |
| 7 | 2.5753 | 2.6137 |
| 8 | 2.5878 | 2.6193 |
| 9 | 2.5762 | 2.6191 |
| 10 | 2.5821 | 2.6117 |
| 11 | 2.6101 | 2.5800 |
| 12 | 2.5756 | 2.6094 |
| 13 | 2.5881 | 2.6001 |
| 14 | 2.5907 | 2.6177 |
| 15 | 2.5910 | 2.6153 |
| 16 | 2.6022 | 2.6130 |

Table 4.8: Cluster Validity Metrics for 2 Principal Components

| Clusters | Partition Coef | CS Index | Separation | Average SSE $* 10^3$ |
|---|---|---|---|---|
| 2 | 0.9031 | $7.4172 * 10^{-4}$ | 5.6178 | 4.1675 |
| 3 | 0.7831 | $7.4472 * 10^{-5}$ | 9.4272 | 2.9941 |
| 4 | 0.7321 | $1.3024 * 10^{-4}$ | 7.1275 | 2.7804 |
| 5 | 0.7057 | $2.4046 * 10^{-5}$ | 5.7659 | 2.5847 |
| 6 | 0.6372 | $4.4011 * 10^{-5}$ | 8.9685 | 2.4750 |
| 7 | 0.6215 | $1.0645 * 10^{-5}$ | 6.9550 | 2.4281 |
| 8 | 0.6111 | $2.2374 * 10^{-4}$ | 4.8516 | 2.4037 |
| 9 | 0.5722 | $5.3835 * 10^{-5}$ | 5.5110 | 2.3972 |
| 10 | 0.5512 | $1.0482 * 10^{-5}$ | 6.8811 | 2.4340 |
| 11 | 0.5284 | $5.6127 * 10^{-5}$ | 8.9179 | 2.4156 |
| 12 | 0.5336 | $1.6353 * 10^{-5}$ | 4.6215 | 2.4262 |
| 13 | 0.5034 | $1.3801 * 10^{-4}$ | 4.1628 | 2.4389 |
| 14 | 0.4892 | $5.7385 * 10^{-5}$ | 5.7243 | 2.4444 |
| 15 | 0.4805 | $6.5907 * 10^{-6}$ | 7.8394 | 2.4760 |
| 16 | 0.4743 | $4.1956 * 10^{-5}$ | 7.8047 | 2.4524 |

The ordering of cluster centers and change centroids was again compared for each of the two principal components in Table 4.9. Note that the first principal component again shows a monotonic relationship to the change centroids. The second principal component, which is assumed to be a noise dimension, does not show a monotonic relationship to the change centroids. The average SSE obtained using two principal components was also compared with that obtained by using three principal components. Using three principal components increases the SSE considerably (see Table 4.10). These two tables support the notion that there is only one principal dimension in the MIS dataset. Furthermore, this single dimension again shows a monotonic relationship to the change centroids. This evidence supports our earlier finding, that the metrics in the MIS dataset are monotonically related to the change counts per module.

Table 4.9: Ordering of PCA Cluster Centers by Attribute

| Attribute | Ordering of Clusters |
|---|---|
| Principal Component #1 | 2, 3, 4, 5, 7, 9, 8, 1, 6 |
| Principal Component #2 | 8, 6, 2, 9, 5, 3, 4, 7, 1 |
| **Change Centroids** | 2, 3, 4, 5, 7, 9, 8, 1, 6 |

Table 4.10: Average SSE for 2 vs. 3 Principal Components

| Clusters | Average SSE * $10^3$ – 2 Principal Components | Average SSE * $10^3$ – 3 Principal Components |
|---|---|---|
| 2 | 4.1675 | 4.7424 |
| 3 | 2.9941 | 3.2418 |
| 4 | 2.7804 | 3.0138 |
| 5 | 2.5847 | 2.9945 |
| 6 | 2.4750 | 2.8689 |
| 7 | 2.4281 | 2.8594 |
| 8 | 2.4037 | 2.8519 |
| 9 | 2.3972 | 2.8857 |
| 10 | 2.4340 | 2.8959 |
| 11 | 2.4156 | 2.8203 |
| 12 | 2.4262 | 2.8268 |
| 13 | 2.4389 | 2.8516 |
| 14 | 2.4444 | 2.8510 |
| 15 | 2.4760 | 2.8933 |
| 16 | 2.4524 | 2.8626 |

### 4.4.2 Results for the ProcSoft Dataset

Since the ProcSoft dataset does not include change counts, the average SSE metric from Section 4.1 is unusable. Instead, only the partition coefficient, the CS index, and the Separation index are used as cluster validity metrics. The number of clusters varied from 2 to 10. The metrics for each partition are given in Table 4.11.

Table 4.11: Cluster Validity Metrics for ProcSoft

| Clusters | Partition Coef | CS Index | Separation Index |
|:---:|:---:|:---:|:---:|
| 2 | 0.8795 | 0.0012 | 20.0554 |
| 3 | 0.7524 | $1.4633 * 10^{-4}$ | 39.6065 |
| 4 | 0.6951 | $3.4166 * 10^{-4}$ | 21.4158 |
| 5 | 0.6138 | $4.2281 * 10^{-5}$ | 33.1550 |
| 6 | 0.5450 | $1.5024 * 10^{-4}$ | 35.7366 |
| 7 | 0.5392 | $2.3218 * 10^{-4}$ | 13.5172 |
| 8 | 0.5070 | $1.1190 * 10^{-4}$ | 12.8757 |
| 9 | 0.4738 | $1.7293 * 10^{-4}$ | 13.0638 |
| 10 | 0.4416 | $3.1477 * 10^{-4}$ | 19.4462 |

As can be seen, the partition coefficient and the CS index both indicate that two clusters is the optimal number, while the Separation index indicates that eight clusters is the optimal number. The ordering of cluster centers amongst these metrics again shows a monotonic relationship between these attributes, as can be seen in Table 4.12. While this table does not provide a final answer on which partition is superior, is does hint quite strongly that the ProcSoft dataset appears to again be monotonic in nature. This result is supported by a PCA analysis, which again shows that there is a single principal component to the ProcSoft dataset. This result is again different from the pairwise linear correlation analysis in [52]; that analysis indicated that the Lines of Comments attribute was only strongly correlated to the Lines of Code attribute.

Additional information may be obtained by examining Tables 4.13 and 4.14, which show the size of each cluster (i.e. how many patterns have the highest degree of membership in this cluster). Notice that for two clusters, the distribution of patterns is skewed towards cluster two, which contains larger metrics values, while the distribution is skewed towards clusters of smaller values when we have an eight-cluster partition. Comparing these results to Table 4.18, where a statistical characterization of the entire dataset is presented, one sees that the proper skew in this dataset is indeed towards smaller values. Thus, the partition into eight clusters will be the most representative.

Table 4.12: Ordering of Cluster Centers by Attribute

| Attributes | Ordering – 2 Clusters | Ordering – 8 Clusters |
|---|---|---|
| Halstead's n1 | 1, 2 | 2, 5, 7, 4, 6, 8, 3, 1 |
| Halstead's n2 | 1, 2 | 2, 5, 7, 4, 6, 8, 3, 1 |
| Halstead's N1 | 1, 2 | 2, 5, 7, 4, 6, 8, 3, 1 |
| Halstead's N2 | 1, 2 | 2, 5, 7, 4, 6, 8, 3, 1 |
| Halstead's N | 1, 2 | 2, 5, 7, 4, 6, 8, 3, 1 |
| Halstead's N^ | 1, 2 | 2, 5, 7, 4, 6, 8, 3, 1 |
| Jensen's NF | 1, 2 | 2, 5, 7, 4, 6, 8, 3, 1 |
| McCabe's VG1 | 1, 2 | 2, 5, 7, 4, 6, 8, 3, 1 |
| McCabe enhanced – VG2 | 1, 2 | 2, 5, 7, 4, 6, 8, 3, 1 |
| Lines of Code | 1, 2 | 2, 5, 7, 4, 6, 8, 3, 1 |
| Lines of Comments | 1, 2 | 2, 5, 7, 4, 6, 8, 3, 1 |

Table 4.13: Cluster Size for 8-Partition

| Cluster | Partition |
|---|---|
| 2 | 82 |
| 5 | 136 |
| 7 | 83 |
| 4 | 59 |
| 6 | 23 |
| 8 | 25 |
| 3 | 11 |
| 1 | 3 |

Table 4.14: Cluster Size for 2-Partition

| Cluster | Patterns |
|---|---|
| 1 | 59 |
| 2 | 363 |

### 4.4.3 Results for OOSoft

As with the ProcSoft dataset, change counts are not included in the OOSoft dataset. Thus, the partition coefficient, the CS index and the Separation index are once again relied upon as validity metrics. The values of these metrics are presented in Table 4.15 for partitions of 2 to 10 clusters.

Table 4.15: Cluster Validity Metrics for OOSoft

| Clusters | Partition Coef | CS Index | Separation Index |
|:---:|:---:|:---:|:---:|
| 2 | 0.7371 | $1.0164 * 10^{-4}$ | 229.2901 |
| 3 | 0.6601 | $3.1147 * 10^{-4}$ | 184.2069 |
| 4 | 0.6704 | $3.1147 * 10^{-4}$ | 95.8886 |
| 5 | 0.6695 | $6.9479 * 10^{-4}$ | 8.9305 |
| 6 | 0.5938 | $4.9494 * 10^{-4}$ | 16.0950 |
| 7 | 0.5383 | $4.1993 * 10^{-4}$ | 17.9859 |
| 8 | 0.5150 | $1.0724 * 10^{-4}$ | 17.2931 |
| 9 | 0.5037 | $6.4591 * 10^{-4}$ | 16.1833 |
| 10 | 0.4767 | $6.4591 * 10^{-4}$ | 17.8566 |

Table 4.16: Cluster Center Orderings for OOSoft

| Feature | Cluster Center Ordering |
|:---:|:---:|
| n1 | 1, 3, 2, 4, 5 |
| n2 | 1, 3, 2, 4, 5 |
| N1 | 1, 3, 2, 4, 5 |
| N2 | 1, 3, 2, 4, 5 |
| N | 1, 3, 2, 4, 5 |
| Nh | 1, 3, 2, 4, 5 |
| Nf | 1, 3, 2, 4, 5 |
| McCabe1 | 1, 3, 2, 4, 5 |
| McCabe2 | 1, 3, 2, 4, 5 |
| LOC | 1, 2, 4, 3, 5 |
| Comments | 1, 2, 4, 5, 3 |

Both the CS index and the Separation index show a global extremum at five clusters. The cluster center orderings this time did *not* indicate a purely monotonic relationship amongst all the metrics. As can be seen in

Table 4.16, all metrics save the Lines of Code and the Lines of Comments are monotonically related. However, the Lines of Code and Lines of Comments are not monotonically related to the others, and have a limited relationship to each other. As with the MIS and ProcSoft datasets, a PCA analysis shows that there is only one principal dimension. The fact that the Lines of Code and Lines of Comments are substantially different from the other metrics was determined by DeVilbiss in [52].

The differences between ProcSoft and OOSoft deserve some comment. Both datasets were extracted from similar applications, and the same metrics were recorded for each. However, only in the OOSoft dataset is there a low correlation between LOC or Comments and the rest of the metrics. At this point, it might be instructive to review some of the basic statistics for each of these datasets, which are presented in Tables 4.17 and 4.18. For every single metric, the average, median and maximum values are significantly smaller in the OOSoft dataset than in the ProcSoft dataset. This fact was remarked on in [52]; a thorough analysis showed that much of the complexity of the structured program was due to the use of SWITCH statements to determine the data type of arguments. Clearly, this is unnecessary in object-oriented systems that support polymorphism and overloading. The removal of these SWITCH statements simplifies the program, and reduces the average and median values of the metrics. However, the relative change in the LOC was smaller than the changes for other metrics, while the use of comments in the object-oriented program was significantly different than in the structured program. These observations account for the difference in the clustering results for the ProcSoft and OOSoft datasets; the meaning of these observations is less clear. Without module change data, one cannot conclude that object-oriented methods will be less change-prone than functions in a procedural program. Indeed, the nature of object-oriented programming, which allows multiple methods access to shared data structures in a class, introduces significant opportunities for subtle program errors. In many ways, testing a class is similar to testing a procedural program with a significant number of global variables, in that the class variables produce a complex coupling between different methods in the class. While the removal of unnecessary complexity is helpful, object-oriented systems are not a silver bullet. The complexity savings, and the greater conceptual integrity enforced by object-oriented analysis and design, must be weighed against the increased complexity of testing classes [12, 13].

Table 4.17: Statistics for OOSoft

|  | *Min* | *Max* | *Mean* | *Median* | *STD* |
|---|---|---|---|---|---|
| n1 | 1.00 | 43.00 | 11.53 | 11.00 | 6.74 |
| n2 | 1.00 | 53.00 | 7.81 | 6.00 | 6.92 |
| N1 | 1.00 | 375.00 | 28.17 | 21.50 | 37.12 |
| N2 | 1.00 | 292.00 | 14.96 | 9.00 | 23.92 |
| N | 2.00 | 667.00 | 43.13 | 33.00 | 60.35 |
| Nh | 1.00 | 480.00 | 70.77 | 64.00 | 64.92 |
| Nf | 0.00 | 362.00 | 48.25 | 42.00 | 47.52 |
| McC1 | 1.00 | 28.00 | 2.27 | 2.00 | 2.59 |
| McC2 | 1.00 | 36.00 | 2.49 | 2.00 | 3.30 |
| LOC | 14.00 | 387.00 | 56.17 | 40.00 | 49.50 |
| CMT | 2.00 | 299.00 | 36.60 | 21.00 | 42.89 |

Table 4.18: Statistics for ProcSoft

|  | *Min* | *Max* | *Mean* | *Median* | *STD* |
|---|---|---|---|---|---|
| n1 | 1.00 | 54.00 | 16.48 | 15.00 | 9.52 |
| n2 | 1.00 | 151.00 | 17.91 | 12.00 | 18.94 |
| N1 | 1.00 | 884.00 | 75.28 | 37.00 | 110.17 |
| N2 | 1.00 | 498.00 | 44.80 | 20.50 | 68.60 |
| N | 2.00 | 1303.00 | 120.08 | 56.50 | 178.10 |
| Nh | 1.00 | 1292.00 | 155.78 | 101.50 | 170.66 |
| Nf | 0.00 | 1029.00 | 112.48 | 69.50 | 132.47 |
| McC1 | 1.00 | 67.00 | 5.39 | 3.00 | 6.87 |
| McC2 | 1.00 | 72.00 | 6.12 | 3.00 | 7.87 |
| LOC | 3.00 | 786.00 | 84.92 | 55.00 | 92.83 |
| CMT | 0.00 | 524.00 | 51.07 | 34.00 | 60.27 |

### *4.4.4 Conclusions from Fuzzy Clustering*

As noted in the preceding sections, a distinguishing feature of the MIS, OOSoft and ProcSoft datasets is that they are one-dimensional and monotonic in nature. In the MIS and ProcSoft datasets, all metrics showed this monotonic relationship to each other, while all but the LOC and Comments in OOSoft were monotonically related. In addition, the MIS dataset shows a monotonic relationship between each metric and the number of changes in the module. This phenomenon is referred to as *multicollinearity*, and it has been repeatedly highlighted in the literature as one of the most challenging features of software metric datasets. Quite simply, multicollinearity tends to confound statistical regression models. Indeed, one of the main motivations for using Principal Component Analysis in previous studies was to avoid the multicollinearity of metrics, since it is a common feature of software metric datasets.

Three further points can be highlighted concerning the MIS dataset. First, Bandwidth is indeed a useful program metric. It bears a similar relationship to software changes that other metrics do, and its removal from this dataset has a clear, negative effect on the clustering results, contradicting the results from [166, 167]. Second, the dataset is actually quite noisy. The divergence of the general cluster validity measures from the tenfold cross-validation results shows that the partitions having the classically "best" cluster quality do not actually represent this dataset. We believe this to be a problem of under-determination; the set of metrics in this experiment truly does not quantify the full "state of nature" in software systems. While this result is well known in the context of regression analysis, its confirmation through machine learning techniques is a notable result. Finally, in addition to the familiar problem of skewness, this investigation also pointed out another unwelcome statistical characteristic: *variance.* Variance also complicates regression analysis and machine learning. The clusters detected in the MIS dataset show a monotonic relationship between increasing mean change values and increasing change variance. Thus, the clusters with the highest change rates (the ones we are most interested in) also have the highest variance.

## 4.5 Data Mining

In this section, the same three datasets are analyzed using data mining tools available on the Web. The Info-Fuzzy Network (IFN) [155] was developed by Mark Last and is described in [176]. This data mining tool uses information-theoretic algorithms to extract IF-THEN rules from a database, and has been used in various data mining tasks, including medical data mining [157] and quality control in the semiconductor industry [156]. These IF-THEN rules may be positive associations, or they might be negative associations (i.e. negative rules). The IFN can only be used in cases where there is a target attribute, and so is applied solely to the MIS dataset in this paper. To conduct data mining on the OOSoft and ProcSoft datasets, the WizRule tool [298] created by the WizSoft corporation is used. This tool searches for associations in a table of data, without the need to specify a target attribute. Both of these tools are rule-extraction algorithms, which means they search for cause-and-effect relationships in the data, and present those relationships in the form of linguistic (IF-THEN) rules In terms of the knowledge discovery process discussed in Chapter 1, these tools both perform data mining and enable the user to evaluate and consolidate the results of data mining.

### *4.5.1 The MIS Dataset*

The IFN is a data mining tool for data tables in which there is a target attribute – an attribute whose value is to be predicted by the remaining attributes, which become inputs. The IFN works by aggregating values in each attribute domain into groups, and then performing data mining over those groups. Thus, rules extracted by the IFN always deal with *intervals* of data, rather than individual data points. The IFN discretizes all input attributes, and assumes that the target attribute is in some discrete form (i.e. classes). Thus, the first step in data mining in the MIS dataset is to transform the change-count attribute into class information. This is done by using the hardened classes from Section 4.1. These classes become the values of the target attribute in the data mining process. A minimum confidence level of 95% was specified for the rules extracted by the IFN.

---

IF Code_Chars is [30, 349] THEN Class = 4
IF Code_Chars is [30,349] THEN Class IS NOT 4
IF Code_Chars is [524, 754] THEN Class = 1
IF Code_Chars is [524, 754] THEN Class IS NOT 4
IF Code_Chars is [1841, 2221] THEN Class = 6
IF Code_Chars is [1841, 2221] THEN Class = 7
IF Code_Chars is [2221, 2762] THEN Class IS NOT 6
IF Code_Chars is [2221, 2762] THEN Class = 7
IF Code_Chars > 7547 THEN Class = 5
IF Code_Chars is [349, 524] and LOC is [3, 57] THEN Class IS NOT 1
IF Code_Chars is [349, 524] and LOC is [3, 57] THEN Class = 4
IF Code_Chars is [349, 524] and LOC is [57, 89] THEN Class = 1
IF Code_Chars is [349, 524] and LOC is [57, 89] THEN Class IS NOT 4
IF Code_Chars is [349, 524] and LOC is [89, 209] THEN Class = 1
IF Code_Chars is [754, 1201] and LOC is [3, 57] THEN Class = 1
IF Code_Chars is [754, 1201] and LOC is [3, 57] THEN Class IS NOT 4
IF Code_Chars is [754, 1201] and LOC is [57, 89] THEN Class = 1
IF Code_Chars is [1201, 1841] and LOC is [57, 89] THEN Class = 1
IF Code_Chars is [1201, 1841] and LOC is [57, 89] THEN Class = 6
IF Code_Chars is [1201, 1841] and LOC is [89, 209] THEN Class IS NOT 1
IF Code_Chars is [1201, 1841] and LOC is [89, 209] THEN Class = 6
IF Code_Chars is [1201, 1841] and LOC is [89, 209] THEN Class IS NOT 7
IF Code_Chars is [2762, 4638] and LOC is [89, 209] THEN Class IS NOT 6
IF Code_Chars is [2762, 4638] and LOC is [89, 209] THEN Class = 7
IF Code_Chars is [4638, 7547] and LOC is [209, 471] THEN Class = 2
IF Code_Chars is [4638, 7547] and LOC is [209, 471] THEN Class = 3
IF Code_Chars is [4638, 7547] and LOC is > 471 THEN Class = 3
IF Code_Chars is [4638, 7547] and LOC is > 471 THEN Class = 5
IF Code_Chars is [754, 1201] and LOC is [89, 209] and NF is [0.8, 178.9] THEN Class = 1
IF Code_Chars is [754, 1201] and LOC is [89, 209] and NF is [0.8, 178.9] THEN Class IS NOT 6
IF Code_Chars is [754, 1201] and LOC is [89, 209] and NF is [178.9, 465.9] THEN Class IS NOT 1
IF Code_Chars is [754, 1201] and LOC is [89, 209] and NF is [178.9, 465.9] THEN Class = 6
IF Code_Chars is [2762,4638] and LOC is [209,471] and NF is [178.9,465.9] THEN Class = 7
IF Code_Chars is [2762,4638] and LOC is [209,471] and NF is > 465.9 THEN Class IS NOT 2
IF Code_Chars is [2762,4638] and LOC is [209,471] and NF is > 465.9 THEN Class = 3

---

Figure 4.2: Rules from IFN

A total of 35 rules, both positive and negative, were extracted from this dataset (see Figure 4.2). In general, these rules support the earlier assertion that the dataset is monotonic in nature; the metric values and the change classes tend to increase in unison with each other. The most interesting result of this data mining experiment is the set of attributes that were found to be significant predictors of the change class. As can be seen, only the total lines of source code, the number of code characters, and the NF estimator of Halstead's N were determined to be significant. Referring to Section 4.3, Table 1, these are *not* in any way the most correlated with the total number of changes. Indeed, the attribute with the single highest correlation to the change counts (Comments) is not seen as significant at all, and only one of the three attributes with the highest correlation to the change counts (Total lines of source code) is seen as significant.

### 4.5.2 The OOSoft Dataset

As discussed earlier, the OOSoft dataset does not contain change data. As a result, there is no target attribute, and the IFN algorithm is not applicable. However, another data mining tool called WizRule is able to search for associations in a table of data even when there is no target attribute. As with IFN, the output of WizRule is a sequence of IF-THEN rules. However, in the case of WizRule, there is no separation into input and target attributes. All attributes may at times appear in the antecedent of a rule or in the consequent of a rule. While this format enables data mining in the absence of a target attribute, it does tend to generate a large number of rules for each *association* that is found. In addition, WizRule will use both intervals and individual data points in its rules. However, there are no negative rules in WizRule.

To minimize the number of rules, the rule probability threshold was set as high as possible (99%). However, the extreme skewness of this dataset complicated the data mining efforts. One of the parameters of WizRule is the minimum number of records in which a rule must be present in order to be extracted. Lowering this threshold can rapidly increase the number of extracted rules. With the deep skewness of the OOSoft dataset, this threshold was ten records. These parameters caused WizRule to extract 795 IF-THEN rules from the 562 records in OOSoft.

The bulk of the rules extracted by WizRule described one of three associations: 1) that small values of some metrics implied a small value of another metric; 2) that large values of some metrics implied a large value for another metric; 3) that the Halstead family of metrics are strongly related to each other. Plainly, these are associations that were already observed. However, there were a few other associations that came to light, which were less obvious. As an example, 43 of the rules extracted from OOSoft represent an association between a specific value for each of the different metrics. However, this information had to be determined through a manual inspection of the rules; it was not presented as a single, cohesive association, and the meaning of this association is unclear. A few other, similar associations may be found in the rules as well. However, the sheer number of rules produced makes it difficult to extract interesting information from the data mining results.

### 4.5.3 The ProcSoft Dataset

As with OOSoft, WizRule was used to conduct data mining in the ProcSoft dataset. Again, the threshold number of records was set to 10 (since ProcSoft is also skewed), while the significance threshold was set to 99%. This resulted in the generation of 200 rules, most of which described the association of small values with small values, large values with large values, and Halstead metrics with each other. However, a few more interesting rules were also found. In particular, there were instances when metric values that were less than the largest range were associated with the largest ranges of other metrics. For instance, the rule

IF n1=[30, 54] and McCabe=[15, 67] THEN McCabe2=[18, 72]

relates the largest values of the n1, McCabe and McCabe2 metrics together. However, the rule

IF McCabe2=[18, 45] and CMT=[137, 422] THEN LOC=[247, 786]

relates a lower value of McCabe2 to the maximum values of CMT and LOC. Again, these more interesting cases had to be determined by manual inspection. They are nonetheless worthwhile, since they signal behaviors that are somewhat unexpected.

## 4.6 Remarks

This investigation has for the first time combined fuzzy clustering and data mining for the analysis of software metrics data. This work provides a new perspective on these three datasets, and points the way toward the use of data mining technology in the context of software process control. For organizations at the higher levels of the Capability Maturity Model, there is a need to analyze software quality data and apply this information to process improvement activities. This study points out the need to rely on more than just a correlation analysis for this purpose; the more powerful techniques of machine learning and data mining are important, useful tools for software quality analysis.

Some of the special challenges that are a characteristic of this application domain were highlighted in this study. Firstly, the individual metric values and the change rates for a module all tend to be highly correlated with each other. This is a phenomenon known as *multicollinearity*, and it is a serious problem for most data analysis techniques. Most statistical regression models assume independence between the predictor attributes, which is clearly not the case. Machine learning algorithms are able to operate in the presence of multicollinearity, but their results can also be subtly affected. In general, small variations from the overriding linear behavior would be discarded as noise, when in fact those might be the most interesting features. One of the main motivations for using PCA in software metrics research is that each eigenvector thus obtained is orthogonal to every other eigenvector, and thus individual attributes in the reduced feature space are in fact independent of one another.

A second major characteristic is skewness. As mentioned, and as was demonstrated in the clustering experiments on the MIS dataset, software metric datasets tend to be skewed towards modules with low metric values and low change rates. Machine learning algorithms tend to be less effective at identifying minority classes in a skewed dataset. To this fact, these experiments also added another complication: the change distributions in modules with high metric values also seem to have larger variation. This result comes from the MIS experiments; the sample standard deviation of the changes in a cluster appeared to be monotonic increasing with the mean of the changes in the cluster. This will complicate machine learning in general, and be a very serious problem for *function approximation* approaches in particular. Classification approaches will also be affected, but the coarser granularity of the dependent variable in will mitigate the impact of the higher variance.

A third characteristic of software metric datasets is that they are underdetermined. As industrial experience and these experiments have shown, a single metric or a combination of metrics is not a complete predictor of the changes in a module. This is again a subtle problem for machine learning approaches, which implicitly assume that each input-output pattern is a sample of a function. In other words, machine learning algorithms assume that the input component of a pattern contains the values of all independent variables from the true mapping between inputs and outputs. The experiments with the MIS dataset showed a clear difference between the usual cluster validity measures and the predictive accuracy of those clusters, indicating a significant departure from this assumption.

Chapter 5 revisits the three datasets explored in this chapter, and examines ways to remove or overcome the skewness present in them. The technique that will be used is called resampling, and is commonly used in the machine learning community. However, to the best of the author's knowledge, resampling has never been used in the software quality domain before. Resampling a dataset can homogenize the class distribution in that dataset, allowing a more effective investigation of minority classes. In the software metrics domain, this means that resampling can improve a classifier's ability to recognize the relatively few modules with large metric values and a high change rate.

# Chapter 5

# Skewness and Resampling

## 5.1 Introduction

As discussed in the previous chapter, software metrics are used to measure the current quality of a software system. While there appears to be an overall linear relationship between metric values and failure rates, this relationship is not fully understood. At this point, a module with a McCabe's complexity of 20 seems much more likely to fail than one with a McCabe's complexity of 5; however, software engineers cannot quantify this assertion. Quite simply, none of the hundreds of software metrics available are adequate predictors of future failure rates. Furthermore, the use of multiple metrics is complicated by the fact that metrics are linearly related to *each other*, as well as to the failure rate. This phenomenon of *multicollinearity* renders statistical regression useless, since independence among regressor variables is a fundamental assumption of the regression algorithms.

Machine learning algorithms, on the other hand, are able to operate in the presence of multicollinearity, as demonstrated in [7, 47, 67, 138, 141], among others. However, machine learning suffers from a different problem: databases of metrics for any project are heavily skewed towards modules with low metric values and low failure rates. Skewness distorts a machine learning algorithm because the algorithm is attempting to optimize a global performance index. For instance, if a particular dataset contains 95% small, safe modules and 5% risky models, a machine learner can simply guess that the module is small and safe – and thereby achieve an accuracy of 95%, which is considered very high [36]. Since the data themselves are skewed, the model a machine learns from these data is also skewed. This is a serious problem because the instances developers want to learn about – the high-risk modules – are not being given priority by the learner.

Skewed datasets are not new to the machine learning community. The primary approaches to dealing with skewness are to resample the dataset, or to penalize the learner for not recognizing minority-class examples. In resampling, instead of simply taking the dataset as given, one can preprocess it so that the interesting cases form a majority of the training data. This can be accomplished by undersampling the majority class, oversampling the minority class, or both. Alternatively, a learner can be penalized by modifying the global performance index to include a cost for each error. The cost per error can be higher for minority-class examples, and can thus force the learner to make fewer mistakes on minority-class examples. Interestingly, the only attempt to deal with skewness in the domain of software metrics has been to use differing misclassification penalties in a decision tree algorithm [139]. The investigation in this chapter applies a new resampling algorithm, SMOTE [36], to the problem of skewness in metrics datasets. The C4.5 decision tree learner [245] is then used to mine the resampled datasets. When the resulting trees are compared against the trees generated from the original datasets, the trees from resampled datasets identified risky modules more accurately than trees from the original datasets.

The remainder of this chapter is organized as follows. In Section 2, the existing literature on machine learning in skewed databases is reviewed. Experimental results from the resampled datasets are presented and compared to the original datasets in Section 3. Ideas on how to use these results in a practical setting are discussed in Section 4.

## 5.2 Machine Learning in Skewed Datasets

In many interesting machine learning problems, objects are not homogeneously distributed among the different classes. Very often, the available data mostly consist of predominantly "normal" examples, with only a few "abnormal" examples. The abnormal examples, however, are precisely the ones that are most interesting to analysts. In addition, when there are costs to misclassifying an example, the cost of mistaking an "abnormal" example for a "normal" example is often much higher than classifying a "normal" example as "abnormal." The problem this poses is that a machine-learning algorithm usually works by defining some global performance index to rate the algorithm's current representation of a given problem. Learning then involves changing the problem representation to optimize that global index. This may involve adding new branches to a tree, updating connection weights in a neural network, producing a new generation of solutions in a genetic algorithm, adding or modifying rules in an expert system, etc. Clearly, when the "abnormal" cases are just a tiny fraction of the population, they cannot have a very large effect on the global index, and will thus be ignored to some extent by the learner [36].

The machine learning community has used several different approaches to overcome skewness in a dataset. The two most common are misclassification penalties and resampling techniques. Misclassification penalties are used to "punish" a learning algorithm when it makes an error. By associating a different penalty with different types of mistakes, the user can force a learner to avoid certain kinds of mistakes, at the cost of making more errors of a different type. Thus, mistaking an "abnormal" case for a "normal" one might carry a higher penalty than mistaking a "normal" case for an "abnormal" one, or vice versa. The precise penalty strategy depends on the problem domain and the user's goals. Misclassification penalties are an option in CART trees, and can be implemented for a variety of machine learning algorithms through post-processing [56, 228].

Resampling is the other major technique for dealing with skewed datasets. Resampling in this sense is distinct from bagging or boosting. Bagging is a resampling technique intended to perturb a learner; a dataset is sampled *with replacement* to create a new dataset of the same size. This dataset is, properly speaking, not a set, since it can contain repeated elements. It is instead known as a *bag*. Plainly, the class distribution in the bag will be roughly the same as in the original dataset. A collection of such bags is formed, and then an ensemble of classifiers is trained on the resulting bags, one classifier to each bag. The set of test inputs is then submitted to the ensemble, which votes on the final classification for each input. The combination of bagging and voting is usually superior to creating a single classifier, provided that the learning algorithm is unstable [28]. Boosting is another technique for creating classifier ensembles. Boosting algorithms such as AdaBoost [264] sequentially train classifiers, placing more emphasis on certain patterns in each successive iteration. This is done by defining a probability density over the training data. For learning algorithms that do not support weighted training patterns, the same effect can be achieved by resampling the dataset with replacement, according to the desired probability density. This is the primary difference between boosting and bagging, since bagging uses *uniform* sampling with replacement.

The resampling techniques of interest in this study are also referred to as *stratification*. They are used to alter the class distributions within a dataset, either to homogenize them or to make the classifier more sensitive to misclassification costs (as mentioned in [56]). The simplest approach is under-sampling, wherein a subset of majority-class examples is randomly selected for inclusion in the resampled dataset *without* replacement. This effectively thins out the majority class, making the dataset more homogenous. Similarly, a simple over-sampling approach would be to duplicate examples from the minority class and include them in the resampled dataset [36]. More advanced techniques are also available in the literature; for instance, an under-sampling technique that preserves the class boundaries in a dataset is used in [150]. This is accomplished using the concept of Tomek links from statistical theory. In another vein, the SMOTE algorithm [36] creates *synthetic* examples in the minority class to be added to the genuine examples in the minority class. This is an over-sampling technique that was originally motivated by decision-tree learning. The authors found that simply replicating examples from the minority class causes decision trees to construct a small, tightly focused decision region around the replicated examples. As an alternative, the authors created synthetic examples along the line in feature space that connects a minority class example to its nearest neighbor in the same class. They found that this approach resulted in an expanded decision region, and thus better generalization. A somewhat different application of under-sampling is the "uncertainty sampling" technique in [161]. The problem area in that paper is automatically labeling unlabelled examples in datasets; however, skewness also affects any effort to automatically categorize these unlabelled examples.

There are also other approaches to skewed datasets that do not fall under the umbrella of resampling or error penalties. Bayesian networks are often used to represent the probability structure of a dataset, but their performance as classifiers is sometimes suspect. In [71], the authors use classification accuracy as the driving goal in forming a Bayesian network. The resulting network performs well, but is considerably different from a traditional Bayesian network. By contrast, DeRouin and Brown [51] approach neural-network learning for skewed datasets by adding an adaptive *attention factor* to the learning rate of each neuron. The attention factor depends on the class distribution of the dataset, and on the proportion of each class that has already been presented for training.

In addition to methods for overcoming skewness, machine learning researchers have also been investigating the performance measures used to compare different algorithms. The traditional measure, classification error, has been extensively attacked for not incorporating the differing costs of different mistakes, and for not offering a complete picture of the relative performance of two classifiers. Provost and Fawcett [243] have instead argued for the use of the Receiver Operating Characteristic (ROC) curve from signal processing as a superior measure of classifier performance. Other authors have offered their own interpretations of the ROC curve [58], or used the curve itself to create new metrics for classifier performance [27]. A number of metrics are available for the specialized task of evaluating collections of text documents, where classes may be both skewed and sparse [61, 200]. An important point to note is that the ROC curve (and to a large extent the metrics for text search) only measure how well one class is learned. The ROC curve plots the number of "True Positives" versus "False Positives," while the text-search metrics of precision and recall are based on the correct or incorrect placement of examples in a category. A metric that naturally measures a classifier's performance in several classes at once is the geometric mean, given by

$$P = \sqrt[k]{acc_1 \cdot acc_2 \cdot \ldots \cdot acc_k} \tag{5.1}$$

where $acc_i$ is the classification accuracy for class $i$ alone.

## 5.3 Experimental Results

A series of data mining experiments was conducted on the three datasets from Chapter 4 using the C4.5 Decision Tree Generator, release 8. Each experiment was a tenfold cross-validation, with the examples in each partition being selected by a stratified sampling algorithm supplied with C4.5. Thus, each individual partition had the same class distribution as the original dataset. The classes used were the fuzzy clusters discussed in Section 4.4, hardened into classes using the method of maximum membership [110]. For each class of interest, the class testing accuracy was computed by dividing the number of correctly classified test examples for the class through all ten iterations of the cross-validation by the total number of examples in that class. The overall performance in each experiment was determined by taking the geometric mean of the accuracies in the classes of interest, given by

$$P = \sqrt[k]{acc_1 \cdot acc_2 \cdot \ldots \cdot acc_k} \tag{5.2}$$

for the $k$ classes of interest in the dataset. Perfect accuracy for all classes of interest will be reflected by a value of $P = 1$.

Resampling approaches work by identifying one or more classes as being interesting, and then altering the distribution of the dataset to favor those classes, at the expense of uninteresting classes. A resampling strategy that improves the learning of one class will degrade the representation of other classes. Thus, the first task is to identifying those classes that are of interest in the three datasets. For the MIS dataset, the mean number of changes per module in each class is a good starting point. An (admittedly arbitrary) decision was made to identify those modules that belong to any class having an average of more than 10 failures. This yields 4 classes of interest: clusters 2, 3, 5 and 7 (see Table

4.5 in Chapter 4). For the OOSoft and ProcSoft datasets, failure counts are unavailable. Based on the known fact that higher metric values correlate well with higher failure rates, classes in these two datasets that have unusually high metric values were identified by comparing the cluster centers in each dimension with the mean value for the whole dataset in that dimension. The classes of interest in ProcSoft and OOSoft are those clusters whose centers are higher than the mean value for each dimension in at least two dimensions.

Experiments with the original datasets were conducted to obtain baseline data. The overall accuracy, class accuracy, and geometric mean for the MIS, OOSoft and ProcSoft datasets are given in Tables 5.1, 5.2, and 5.3. The classes of interest in the MIS dataset were classes 2, 3, 5, and 7. In OOSoft, the classes of interest are classes 3, 4, 5, and in ProcSoft they were classes 1, 3, 8. In general, the classes with the highest accuracy were the ones that either had the lowest or highest metric values; those classes in between were more difficult to classify.

Table 5.1: Tenfold Cross-Validation Results for MIS

|         | *10-Fold Accuracy* |
|---------|---------|
| Overall | 84.9% |
| Class 1 | 80.39% |
| Class 2 | 80% |
| Class 3 | 77.27% |
| Class 4 | 93.46% |
| Class 5 | 91.67% |
| Class 6 | 88.37% |
| Class 7 | 75.61% |
| **Performance** | 0.8091 |

Following these initial experiments, undersampling and SMOTE were used to alter the class distributions in each dataset. The goal was to trade off decreased accuracy in uninteresting classes for increased accuracy in the ones that were interesting, or to *calibrate* a decision tree to perform best on the classes of interest. In general, uninteresting classes were undersampled to as little as 25% of their original population, and interesting classes oversampled by 100 or 200%. In the terminology of this study, $X\%$ undersampling means a class with $X\%$ of the number of examples in the original class, chosen through random uniform sampling without replacement, is created. *Y%* oversampling means that a class that contains *Y*/100 times as many synthetic examples as there were examples in the original class, *plus* all of the original examples, is created. The experiments followed an iterative, exploratory process, and were terminated when all of the interesting classes had a class accuracy greater than the overall accuracy for the entire dataset.

Table 5.2: Tenfold Cross-Validation Results for OOsoft

|  | *10-Fold Accuracy* |
|---|---|
| Overall | 97.7% |
| Class 1 | 98.97% |
| Class 2 | 98.02% |
| Class 3 | 96.9% |
| Class 4 | 94.89% |
| Class 5 | 100% |
| **Performance** | 0.9724 |

Table 5.3: Tenfold Cross-Validation Results for ProcSoft

|  | *10-Fold Accuracy* |
|---|---|
| Overall | 89.1% |
| Class 1 | 66.67% |
| Class 2 | 95.12% |
| Class 3 | 81.82% |
| Class 4 | 79.66% |
| Class 5 | 95.59% |
| Class 6 | 78.26% |
| Class 7 | 87.95% |
| Class 8 | 76% |
| **Performance** | 0.7456 |

Four resampling experiments were conducted in the MIS dataset. The resampling strategy for each of these experiments is shown in Table 5.4. Table 5.5 presents the overall accuracy, class accuracies, and performance for each of these experiments, again determined through a tenfold cross-validation experiment using C4.5. As can be seen, all of the resampling strategies resulted in improved overall accuracy. One can also observe an improvement in the performance measure as the sampling rate for uninteresting classes is decreased, and increased for interesting classes. The procedure is sensitive to the exact combination of undersampling and oversampling used in the dataset. The optimal strategy appears to be specific to each dataset.

Table 5.4: Resampling Strategies in MIS

| Class | Experiment 1 | Experiment 2 | Experiment 3 | Experiment 4 |
|-------|--------------|--------------|--------------|--------------|
| 1 | 50% under | 50% under | 25% under | 25% under |
| 2 | 100% over | 200% over | 100% over | 200% over |
| 3 | 100% over | 200% over | 200% over | 200% over |
| 4 | 50% under | 50% under | 25% under | 25% under |
| 5 | Unchanged | Unchanged | Unchanged | 100% over |
| 6 | 50% under | 50% under | 50% under | 50% under |
| 7 | 100% over | 100% over | 100% over | 100% over |

Table 5.5: Resampling Results in MIS

| | Experiment 1 | Experiment 2 | Experiment 3 | Experiment 4 |
|-------|--------------|--------------|--------------|--------------|
| Overall | 90.4% | 88.9% | 89.8% | 89% |
| Class 1 | 88.24% | 84.31% | 80.77% | 50% |
| Class 2 | 90.0% | 88.33% | 85% | 96.67% |
| Class 3 | 88.64% | 93.94% | 98.48% | 96.97% |
| Class 4 | 94.4% | 87.04% | 92.59% | 74.07% |
| Class 5 | 100% | 91.67% | 91.67% | 95.83% |
| Class 6 | 81.4% | 79.07% | 69.77% | 81.4% |
| Class 7 | 93.9% | 92.68% | 96.34% | 96.34% |
| **Performance** | 0.9303 | 0.9163 | 0.9273 | 0.9645 |

Three resampling experiments were conducted in the OOSoft dataset. The sampling strategy for each experiment is described in Table 5.6, while the results of each experiment are presented in Table 5.7. Similarly, the resampling strategy for the 3 experiments conducted in the ProcSoft dataset is presented in Table 5.8, and the results of those experiments are presented in Table 5.9. As can be seen, the combination of undersampling and SMOTE is consistently able to alter the class accuracies to favor the interesting classes.

Table 5.6: Resampling Strategy for OOSoft

|         | *Experiment 1* | *Experiment 2* | *Experiment 3* |
|---------|----------------|----------------|----------------|
| Class 1 | 50% under      | 50% under      | 25% under      |
| Class 2 | 50% under      | 50% under      | 25% under      |
| Class 3 | Unchanged      | 100% over      | 100% over      |
| Class 4 | Unchanged      | Unchanged      | 100% over      |
| Class 5 | Unchanged      | Unchanged      | Unchanged      |

Table 5.7: Resampling Results for OOSoft

|             | *Experiment 1* | *Experiment 2* | *Experiment 3* |
|-------------|----------------|----------------|----------------|
| Overall     | 96.1%          | 97.2%          | 98.3%          |
| Class 1     | 96.94%         | 98.98%         | 97.96%         |
| Class 2     | 96.15%         | 94.23%         | 94.23%         |
| Class 3     | 86.67%         | 99.17%         | 100%           |
| Class 4     | 94.74%         | 95.79%         | 98.42%         |
| Class 5     | 100%           | 100%           | 100%           |
| **Performance** | 0.9364     | 0.9830         | 0.9947         |

Table 5.8: Resampling Strategy for ProcSoft

|         | *Experiment 1* | *Experiment 2* | *Experiment 3* |
|---------|----------------|----------------|----------------|
| Class 1 | 100% over      | 100% over      | 100% over      |
| Class 2 | 50% under      | 50% under      | 25% under      |
| Class 3 | 100% over      | 200% over      | 200% over      |
| Class 4 | Unchanged      | Unchanged      | Unchanged      |
| Class 5 | 50% under      | 25% under      | 25% under      |
| Class 6 | Unchanged      | Unchanged      | Unchanged      |
| Class 7 | 50% under      | 50% under      | 50% under      |
| Class 8 | 100% over      | 100% over      | 100% over      |

Table 5.9: Resampling Results for ProcSoft

|  | *Experiment 1* | *Experiment 2* | *Experiment 3* |
|---|---|---|---|
| Overall | 87.8% | 87.2% | 89.9% |
| Class 1 | 100% | 100% | 100% |
| Class 2 | 87.8% | 95.12% | 90.48% |
| Class 3 | 86.36% | 93.94% | 96.67% |
| Class 4 | 86.44% | 83.05% | 88.14% |
| Class 5 | 91.18% | 88.23% | 97.06% |
| Class 6 | 69.57% | 73.91% | 78.26% |
| Class 7 | 85.71% | 83.33% | 76.19% |
| Class 8 | 94% | 88% | 92% |
| **Performance** | 0.9329 | 0.9385 | 0.9407 |

## 5.4 Proposed Usage

A classifier, which has been calibrated to identify troublesome modules, will be of great benefit to software developers. Imagine the following scenario: a programmer completes a module for a software system, and checks it in to the configuration control system. A few minutes later, he receives an email telling him that the module he has checked in appears to be in the "moderately risky" category, meaning that there is a higher-than-normal risk of failure in that module, based on the software metrics computed for that module. The programmer then has the opportunity to redesign the module to reduce its complexity, or to prepare a more rigorous testing plan. It is even possible that the project manager might set guidelines for how much testing is needed for each failure risk class. This could be based on a cost optimization model that accounts for the differing levels of risk associated with each risk category. This scenario is the ideal that researchers have been striving for in software metrics research. However, one of the key stumbling blocks is that engineers cannot tell *a priori* what metric values correspond to low risk, medium risk, or high risk categories in a given project. Take McCabe's cyclomatic complexity: one source [275] asserts that a cyclomatic complexity of more than 10 is associated with an increased failure rate, while another [8] might say 15. The real problem is that each development project is in large measure unique. Different team members bring a different set of skills and experience to bear on problems that might be in completely different application areas, and more or less difficult than each other. Notice that even calibrating metrics thresholds from a company's historical data is problematic, since the development team, application domain, and project difficulty are most likely different.

The solution we advocate is to return to an idea proposed by Brooks more than 30 years ago: building a pilot system for each project, with the intent to learn from the pilot system and then *throw it away* [29]. The software development community, for obvious reasons, has not embraced this idea; building a realistic pilot system will be expensive in itself, and thus would significantly increase the cost of software development. However, there are a number of results and observations gathered in the course of decades of software research that point to the usefulness of a pilot system:

i.    Brooks' argument that software development is a learning process certainly rings true. Developers constantly have to learn new application domains to produce products their customers want, application domains that none of the developers may have *any* understanding of. This gap between the domain of software development and the application domain is extremely dangerous [6]. A pilot system will give developers a chance to develop competence in the application domain, before building the production system.

ii.   In his seminal paper describing the waterfall model [254], W. W. Royce *also* argues for the development of a pilot system. His rationale is that matters such as timing and storage allocation should be explored through this pilot system. The developers will be able to experiment with a working system rather than relying on human judgement, which Royce characterizes as "invariably and seriously optimistic" in the area of software development. While timing and storage allocation are no longer the key issues they were in 1970, the underlying principle is the same: design decisions will be sounder if they arise from experimental studies as opposed to human guesses.

iii.  The research on iterative development has showed that rapid prototyping helps determine a user's true requirements, and can lead to better software. Iterative development is now accepted as being far superior to a single, monolithic, design-and-build model. Building a pilot system would certainly fit into the iterative development model.

iv. Other engineering disciplines routinely build pilot systems, and accept the costs as part of the development cycle. No chemical engineer would build a production plant without first building and testing a pilot plant, while manufacturers routinely experiment with process designs before settling on one production process.

v. Finally, the results in Chapter 4 indicate that failure classes are *best* determined through a supervised learning algorithm. While clustering the MIS dataset, and used these clusters to build a decision tree classifier was successful, observe that the cluster partition that best represented the actual failure occurrences was *not* seen as optimal by any of the standard cluster validity metrics. Unsupervised learning is attractive because developers do not have to wait until the system is implemented and tested before data mining can begin; however, the results in Chapter 4 & 5 are evidence that supervised learning is more accurate in this domain, probably due to under-determination of the dataset. If actual failure counts are needed, then only two choices are available: either wait until failure counts become available late in the project (which renders the metrics-based screening process moot), or gather failure data from a pilot system.

There is a general consensus in the software engineering community that software engineers do not fully understand how to produce high-quality software. Engineers have learned that the traditional "waterfall" life cycle is a poor fit to the special characteristics of software development [232], and that some form of iterative process is needed instead. This investigation has pointed out the fact that *there is now a substantial body of evidence that favors building a pilot system as a routine step in software development.* In addition to its other benefits, a pilot system can also be used to calibrate software metrics to the project under development, enabling the construction of automated screening tools for software modules. For those projects that utilize a rapid-prototyping development approach, the tree for the $k$-th filter can be calibrated on the $(k - 1)$-th prototype.

## 5.5 Remarks

This investigation represents the first-ever application of resampling techniques in the domain of software metrics. Resampling has been shown to be a viable technique for calibrating a decision tree to identify classes of interest in a database of software metrics. We suggest that decision-tree calibration can best be carried out through the construction of a pilot system, which should lead to higher-quality software in general. This concludes the experimental portion of this monograph; a summary and discussion of future work are presented in Chapter 6.

# Chapter 6

# Conclusion

Software systems are the most complex technological systems in the world today, and the most ephemeral. They exist as pure information, without any physical component. Software has a reputation for being the most error-prone of all engineering constructs, and yet it is an essential element of the North American infrastructure and economy. This crisis in software quality is probably the most urgent technological challenge of the $21^{st}$ century. At this time, there are no universally accepted models of software reliability, or metrics that can quantify the quality of a software system. Simply put, the understanding of software as an engineered product is still in its infancy.

In this book, we have made three specific contributions to the engineering of software. The first contribution is an experimental investigation of a founding assumption in software reliability modeling. In the literature on software reliability, the idea that software failures are ultimately the result of a stochastic process is a basic assumption. There has never been a specific, empirical study that attempts to support or question this assumption. This investigation, based on best practices in nonlinear time series analysis, shows that software failures actually appear to be deterministic in nature. This result, in itself, is of considerable theoretical importance; it means that the most appropriate software reliability models will be nonlinear, deterministic models, instead of stochastic models. In other words, techniques such as neural networks or fuzzy inferential systems should produce better models of software reliability then non-homogeneous Poisson processes. The underlying causal model proposed for this phenomenon is that the fault set of a program has a fractal geometry. This points the way to a new fault-forecasting technique; if the fault set of a software system is a fractal set as hypothesized, then perhaps the location of unseen faults in a program can be predicted from the location of known faults. This is a potentially significant development in software testing, which will be pursued in future research.

The second contribution is the application of clustering to software metrics analysis. Clustering is an unsupervised learning technique, which means that the algorithm "learns" the distribution of points in some feature space, without needing an *a priori* classification of those points. Clearly, this would be useful in software engineering, where software metrics are available far earlier than failure data. Unsupervised learning algorithms can provide significant insight into what modules pose greater development risks well before failures are observed. In this context, it is quite surprising that fuzzy c-means clustering, a powerful and well-known unsupervised learning algorithm, had not been used in the software metrics domain. The cluster analysis experiments reported in Chapter 4 rectified this omission, and exposed a few new characteristics of software metrics datasets. The most significant of these conclusions has to do with the relationship between the mean number of failures in modules and the variance in failures per module. Quite simply, the groups of modules that have a higher average number of failures also show a higher variance in the number of failures per module. This is very important for any kind of statistical or machine learning algorithm; predictive algorithms will encounter significant difficulties when the variance between classes is not uniform. In particular, the type of machine learning algorithms known as *function approximators* will be severely impacted, as will statistical regression techniques.

The third contribution to software quality has to do with the nature of software metrics datasets. As observed in Chapter 4, and as has been well recorded in the literature, software metrics datasets are heavily skewed. Most modules in a software system are small and have few bugs. Only a few modules are large and buggy. However, it is precisely these large and buggy modules that are most interesting. Learning in skewed datasets is a typical machine learning problem, and two major approaches have been developed for dealing with them. One is to associate differing costs with making errors in majority or minority classes; another is to resample the classes and homogenize the distribution of examples across classes. In the software metrics domain, there is a single paper describing different misclassification costs in software metrics datasets, and none whatsoever describing resampling approaches. Resampling experiments conducted using the results of our clustering experiments in Chapter 4 were described in Chapter 5. A machine learning system (in this case the C4.5 decision tree algorithm) was calibrated to preferentially recognize certain classes of modules that posed a high development risk.

It is suggested that this research should be applied in an iterative development model; at the very least, a pilot system should be built on each software project, and used to calibrate metrics for the full system. In a fully iterative development model, each iteration of the system should be used to calibrate metrics for the next iteration. An automated system that will pre-screen modules as soon as they are checked in to configuration management is envisaged. This system would automatically compare a new module's metrics against a model of potentially troublesome modules, and flag any that seem to have an elevated risk of failure. This might simply be a warning that extra testing is needed, or a manager might assign different levels of necessary testing based on the classification of a module. This could also be a component of a deployment decision framework. Industrial studies will be needed to determine if this is a useful and economically viable concept.

Future work in this area includes industrial studies of a calibrated metrics "filter," and an investigation of the fractal fault set hypothesis, as mentioned above. In addition, several related issues were raised in the course of this study:

i.   Firstly, finding the optimal combination of resampling algorithms and machine learning algorithms as an automatic filter requires more study.

ii.  In a similar vein, one can ask what software reliability models are most useful, given the evidence of determinism we have found. Both of these lines of inquiry must address not just the pure machine-learning question of what algorithm gives the highest accuracy, but also practical questions of how machine learning can be used in software testing, how such algorithms may support a human developer, and in what ways the software developer must alter their processes purely to accommodate a particular tool. Both lines of inquiry will also require the examination of existing and novel machine learning architectures.

iii.    One class of software failures that is currently receiving a large amount of attention is security failures or breaches. If the subset of the fault set representing security breaches also has a fractal geometry, then security breaches might also be predicted.

iv.    Most software reliability models today are based on execution time, rather than the amount of wall-clock time spent in testing, although Musa's calendar-time model does provide a means for converting wall-clock time to execution time. However, open source systems, which are tested by a loose association of interested parties, pose real challenges for current software reliability modeling techniques. Fuzzy sets and rough sets might profitably be used to develop reliability models for open-source systems.

# References

[1] Adelson, B.; Soloway, E., "The role of domain experience in software design," *IEEE Transactions on Software Engineering*, vol. 11 no. 11, November 1985, pp. 1351-1360.

[2] Aiken, M.W., "Using artificial intelligence based system simulation in software reusability," *Software Engineering Notes*, vol. 15 no. 5, October 1990, pp. 23-27.

[3] Alander, J.T.; Mantere, T.; Moghadampour, G., "Testing software response times using a genetic algorithm," in *Proceedings, 3$^{rd}$ Nordic Workshop on Genetic Algorithms and Their Applications*, Helsinki, Finland, August 18-22, 1997, pp. 293-298.

[4] American Institute of Aeronautics and Astronautics, *American National Standard Recommended Practice for Software Reliability*, ANSI/AIAA R-013-1992; February 23, 1993.

[5] The Apache Software Foundation, "Welcome! - The Apache Software Foundation," http://www.apache.org/, 2002.

[6] Arango, G.; Freeman, P., "Modeling knowledge for software development," in *Proceedings of the Third International Workshop on Software Specification and Design*, London, U.K., August 26-27, 1985, pp. 63-66.

[7] Baisch, E.; Bleile, T.; Belschner, R., "A neural fuzzy system to evaluate software development productivity," in *Proceedings of the 1995 IEEE International Conference on Systems, Man and Cybernetics*, 1995, pp. 4603-4608.

[8] Baisch, E.; Liedtke, T., "Comparison of conventional approaches and soft-computing approaches for software quality prediction," in *Proceedings of the 1997 IEEE International Conference on Systems, Man and Cybernetics*, 1997, pp. 1045-1049.

[9] Balzer, R., "A 15 year perspective on automatic programming," *IEEE Transactions on Software Engineering*, vol. 11 no. 11, November 1985, pp. 1257-1268.

[10] Bar-Lev, S.K.; Lavi, I.; Reiser, B., "Bayesian inference for the power law process," *Annals of the Institute of Statistical Mathematics*, vol. 44 no. 4, 1992, pp. 623-639.

[11]  Barstow, D.R., "Domain-specific automatic programming," *IEEE Transactions on Software Engineering*, vol. 11 no. 11, November 1985, pp. 1321-1336.

[12]  Bashir, I.; Goel, A.L.; *Testing Object-Oriented Software: Life Cycle Solutions*, New York: Springer-Verlag, 1999.

[13]  Bashir, I.; Paul, R.A., "Object-oriented integration testing," *Annals of Software Engineering*, vol. 8, 1999, pp. 187-202.

[14]  Basili, V.R.; Rombach, H.D., "Support for comprehensive reuse," *Software Engineering Journal*, vol. 6 no. 5, September 1991, pp. 303-316.

[15]  Beck, K.; Coplien, J.O.; Crocker, R.; Dominick, L.; Meszaros, G.; Paulisch, F.; Vlissides, J., "Industrial experience with design patterns," in *Proceedings, 18th International Conference on Software Engineering*, Berlin, Germany, March 25-29, 1996, pp. 103-114.

[16]  Beck, K., et al., "Manifesto for Agile Software Development," http://www.agilemanifesto.org/, 2001.

[17]  Benington, H.D., "Production of large computer programs," in Proceedings, ONR Symposium on Advanced Programming Methods for Digital Computers, June 1956, pp. 15-27. Reprinted in Proceedings, 9th International Conference on Software Engineering, Monterey, CA, USA, March 30-April 2, 1987, pp. 299-310.

[18]  Bezdek, J.C., Pattern Recognition with Fuzzy Objective Function Algorithms, New York: Plenum Press, 1981.

[19]  Bezdek, J.C., "What is computational intelligence?" in Zurada, J.M.; Marks, R.J.; Robinson, C.J., Eds., *Computational Intelligence: Imitating Life*, New York: IEEE Press, 1994, pp. 1-12.

[20]  Bhattacharya, J., "Detection of Weak Chaos in Infant Respiration," *IEEE Transactions on Systems, Man and Cybernetics, Part B: Cybernetics,* vol. 31 no. 4, August 2001, pp. 637-642.

[21]  Bjorner, D.; Jones, C.B., *The Vienna Development Method. The Meta-language*, Berlin, Germany: Springer-Verlag, 1978.

[22]  Bleile, T.; Baisch, E.; Belschner, R., "Neural fuzzy simulation to gain expert knowledge for the improvement of software development productivity," in *Proceedings, Summer Computer Simulation Conference*, Ottawa, ON, Canada, July 24-26, 1995, pp. 317-322.

[23]  Boehm, B.W., "A spiral model of software development and enhancement," *IEEE Computer,* vol. 21 no. 5, May 1988, pp. 61-72.

[24]  Boehm, B., "Get ready for agile methods, with care," *IEEE Computer,* vol. 35 no. 1, pp. 64-69.

[25]  Bortolan, G.; Pedrycz, W., "Reconstruction problem and information granularity," *IEEE Transactions on Fuzzy Systems,* vol. 5 no. 2, May 1997, pp. 234-248.

[26]  Bowyer, K.W., *Ethics and Computing: Living Responsibly in a Computerized World*, Los Alamitos, CA: IEEE Computer Society Press, 1996.

[27] Bradley, A.P., "The use of the area under the ROC curve in the evaluation of machine learning algorithms," *Pattern Recognition*, vol. 30 no. 7, 1997, pp. 1145-1159.

[28] Breiman, L., "Bagging Predictors," *Technical Report No. 421*, September 1994, Department of Statistics, University of California at Berkeley.

[29] Brooks, F.P., Jr., The Mythical Man-Month: Essays on Software Engineering, Anniversary Edition, Reading, MA: Addison-Wesley Pub. Co., 1995.

[30] Brown, N., "Industrial-strength management strategies," *IEEE Software*, vol. 13 no. 4, July 1996, pp. 94-103.

[31] Bubenko, J.; Rolland, C.; Loucopoulos, P.; DeAntonellis, V., "Facilitating 'fuzzy to formal' requirements modeling," in *Proceedings, 1ˢᵗ International Conference on Requirements Engineering*, Colorado Springs, CO, USA, April 18-22, 1994, pp. 154-157.

[32] Budinsky, F.J.; Finnie, M.A., "Automatic code generation from design patterns," *IBM Systems Journal*, vol. 35 no. 2, 1996, pp. 151-171.

[33] Cai, K.-Y.; Wen, C.-Y.; Zhang, M.-L., "A critical review on software reliability modeling," *Reliability Engineering and System Safety,* vol. 32 no. 3, 1991, pp. 357-371.

[34] Carnegie Mellon University, "SEMA-Maturity Profile," http://www.sei.cmu.edu/sema/profile.html, August 24, 2001.

[35] Chang, Y.-C., "A robust tracking control for chaotic Chua's circuits via fuzzy approach," *IEEE Transactions on Circuits and Systems-I: Fundamental Theory and Applications*, vol. 48 no. 7, July 2001, pp. 889-895.

[36] Chawla, N.V.; Bowyer, K.W.; Hall, L.O.; Kegelmeyer, W.P., "SMOTE: synthetic minority over-sampling technique," *Journal of Artificial Intelligence Research*, vol. 16, June 2002, pp. 321-357.

[37] Chilenski, J.J.; Miller, S.P., "Applicability of modified condition/decision coverage to software testing," *Software Engineering Journal*, vol. 9 no. 5, September 1994, pp. 193-200.

[38] Choi, J.; Choi, B., "Test agent system design," in *Proceedings, IEEE International Conference on Fuzzy Systems*, Seoul, Korea, August 22-25, 1999, pp. 326-331.

[39] Cockburn, A.; Highsmith, J., "Agile software development: the people factor," *IEEE Computer,* vol. 34 no. 11, November 2001, pp. 131-133.

[40] Conger, S., *The New Software Engineering,* Belmont, CA: Wadsworth Pub. Co., 1994.

[41] Connell, J.L.; Shafer, L.B., *Structured Rapid Prototyping*, New York: Yourdon Press, 1989.

[42] Cuena, J., "Contributions to a knowledge oriented view of software design," *Knowledge Oriented Software Design*, vol. A-27, 1993, pp. 51-75.

[43] Currit, P.A.; Dyer, M.; Mills, H.D., "Certifying the reliability of software," *IEEE Transactions on Software Engineering*, vol. 12 no. 1, Jan. 1986, pp. 3-11.

[44] Cybenko, G., "Approximation by superpositions of a sigmoidal function," *Mathematics of Control, Signals and Systems,* vol. 2, 1989, pp. 303-314.

[45] DACS Staff, "DACS Software Reliability Dataset," http://www.dacs.dtic.mil/databases/sled/swrel.shtml, Data & Analysis Center for Software.

[46] Darringer, J.A.; King, J.C., "Applications of symbolic execution to program testing," *IEEE Computer*, vol. 11 no. 4, April 1978, pp. 51-60.

[47] De Almeida, M.A.; Lounis, H.; Melo, W.L., "An investigation on the use of machine learned models for estimating software correctability," *International Journal of Software Engineering and Knowledge Engineering*, vol. 9 no. 5, 1999, pp. 565-593.

[48] Deitel, H.M.; Deitel, P.J., *C: How to Program, 2$^{nd}$ Ed.,*Englewood Cliffs, NJ: Prentice-Hall, 1994.

[49] Dellen, B.; Maurer, F.; Munch, J.; Verlage, M., "Enriching software process support by knowledge-based techniques," *International Journal of Software Engineering and Knowledge Engineering*, vol. 7 no. 2, 1997, pp. 185-215.

[50] DeMillo, R.A.; Lipton, R.J.; Sayward, F.G., "Hints on test data selection: help for the practicing programmer," *IEEE Computer*, vol. 11 no. 4, April 1978, pp. 34-41.

[51] DeRouin, E.; Brown, J., "Neural network training on unequally represented classes," in *Proceedings, Artificial Neural Networks in Engineering Conference*, 1991, pp. 135-140.

[52] DeVilbiss, W., "A Comparison of Software Complexity of Programs Developed Using Structured Techniques and Object-Oriented Techniques," Master's Thesis, University of Wisconsin-Milwaukee, 1993.

[53] Dhar, V.; Stein, R, *Intelligent Decision Support Methods: The Science of Knowledge Work,* Upper Saddle River, NJ: Prentice Hall, 1997.

[54] Dick, S.; Kandel, A., "Granular Computing in Neural Networks," in W. Pedrycz, Ed., *Granular Computing: An Emerging Paradigm,* New York: Physica-Verlag Heidelberg, 2001, pp. 275-305.

[55] Dix, A; Finlay, J.; Abowd, G.; Beale, R., *Human-Computer Interaction, 2$^{nd}$ Ed.,* London, U.K.: Prentice Hall Europe, 1998.

[56] Domingos, P., "MetaCost: a general method for making classifiers cost-sensitive," in *Proceedings, KDD-99,* San Diego, CA, USA, Aug. 15-18, 1999, pp. 155-164.

[57] Doyle, J., "Expert systems and the 'myth' of symbolic reasoning," *IEEE Transactions on Software Engineering*, vol. 11 no. 11, pp. 1386-1390.

[58] Drummond, C.; Holte, R.C., "Explicitly representing expected cost: an alternative to ROC representation," in *Proceedings, KDD-2000*, Boston, MA, USA, August 20-23, 2000, pp. 198-207.

[59] Duda, R.O.; Hart, P.E.; Stork, D.G., *Pattern Classification, 2$^{nd}$ Edition*, New York: John Wiley & Sons, Inc., 2001.

[60] Dudding, L.C.; McQuerry, S.L., "Expert Software Pricer (ESP): an AI/algorithmic approach to software costing," in *Proceedings, WESTEX'87, Western Conference on Expert Systems*, Anaheim, CA, USA, June 2-4, 1987, pp. 190-195.

[61] Dumais, S.; Platt, J.; Heckerman, D., "Inductive learning algorithms and representations for text categorization," in *Proceedings, 1998 ACM Int. Conf. On Information and Knowledge Management*, Bethesda, MD, USA, November 3-7, 1998, pp. 148-155.

[62] Dunham, J.R., "Experiments in software reliability: life-critical applications," *IEEE Transactions on Software Engineering*, vol. 12 no. 1, Jan. 1986, pp. 110-123.

[63] Dunham, J.R.; Finelli, G.B., "Real-time software failure characterization," in *Proceedings of COMPASS '90, 5th Annual Conference on Computer Assurance*, June 25-28, 1990, Gaithersburg, MD, USA, pp. 39-45.

[64] Dunn, J.C., "A Fuzzy Relative of the ISODATA Process and its Use in Detecting Compact Well-Separated Clusters," *Journal of Cybernetics*, vol. 3 no. 3, 1973, pp. 32-57. Reprinted in Bezdek, J.C.; Pal, S.K., *Fuzzy Models for Pattern Recognition: Methods that Search for Structures in Data*, Piscataway, NJ: IEEE Press, 1992, pp. 82-101.

[65] Duran, J.W.; Ntafos, S.C., "An evaluation of random testing," *IEEE Transactions on Software Engineering*, vol. 10 no. 4, July 1980, pp. 438-444.

[66] Duran, J.W.; Wiorkowski, J.J., "Quantifying software validity by sampling," *IEEE Transactions on Reliability*, vol. 29 no. 2, June 1980, pp. 141-144.

[67] Ebert, C., "Fuzzy classification for software criticality analysis," *Expert Systems with Applications*, vol. 11 no. 3, pp. 323-342, 1996.

[68] Ebert, C.; Baisch, E., "Knowledge-based techniques for software quality management," in W. Pedrycz, W.; Peters, J.F., Eds., *Computational Intelligence in Software Engineering*, River Edge, NJ: World Scientific, 1998, pp. 295-320.

[69] Eisenstadt, M., "My hairiest bug war stories," *Communications of the ACM*, vol. 40 no. 4, April 1997, pp. 30-37.

[70] Everett, W.W.; Musa, J.D., "A software engineering practice," *IEEE Computer*, vol. 26 no. 3, March 1993, pp. 77-79.

[71] Ezawa, K.J.; Singh, M.; Norton, S.W., "Learning goal oriented Bayesian networks for telecommunications risk management," in *Proceedings, 13th Int. Conf. On Machine Learning*, Bari, Italy, July 3-6, 1996, pp. 139-147.

[72] Fairley, R.E., "Tutorial: static analysis and dynamic testing of computer software," *IEEE Computer*, vol. 11 no. 4, April 1978, pp. 14-23.

[73] Farr, W., "Software Reliability Modeling Survey," in Lyu, M.R., Ed., *Handbook of Software Reliability Engineering*, New York: McGraw-Hill, 1996, pp. 71-115.

[74] Fayyad, U.M., "Data mining and knowledge discovery: Making sense out of data," *IEEE Expert*, vol. 11 no. 5, Oct. 1996, pp. 20-25.

[75] Fickas, S.F., "Automating the transformational development of software," *IEEE Transactions on Software Engineering*, vol. 11 no. 11, November 1985, pp. 1268-1277.

[76] Finelli, G.B., "NASA software failure characterization experiments," *Reliability Engineering and System Safety*, vol. 32 no. 1-2, 1991, pp. 155-169.

[77] Finnie, G.R.; Wittig, G.E., "AI tools for software development estimation," in *Proceedings, 1996 International Conference on Software Engineering: Education and Practice*, Dunedin, New Zealand, January 24-27, 1996, pp. 346-353.

[78] Fleyshgakker, V.N.; Weiss, S.N., "Efficient mutation analysis: a new approach," *Proceedings, ISSTA'94 – International Symposium on Software Testing and Analysis*, Seattle, WA, USA, August 17-19, 1994, pp. 185-195.

[79] Florijn, G.; Meijers, M.; van Winsen, P., "Tool support for object-oriented patterns," in *Proceedings, ECOOP'97 – Object-Oriented Programming*, Jyvaskyla, Finland, June 9-13, 1997, pp. 472-495.

[80] Forman, E.H.; Singpurwalla, N.D., "Optimal time intervals for testing hypotheses on computer software errors," *IEEE Transactions on Reliability*, vol. 28 no. 3, Aug. 1979, pp. 250-253.

[81] Frankl, P.G.; Weyuker, E.J., "An applicable family of data flow testing criteria," *IEEE Transactions on Software Engineering*, vol. 14 no. 10, October 1988, pp. 1483-1498.

[82] Frankl, P.G.; Weyuker, E.J., "A formal analysis of the fault-detecting ability of testing methods," *IEEE Transactions on Software Engineering*, vol. 19 no. 3, March 1993, pp. 202-213.

[83] Free Software Foundation, Inc., "Free Software Foundation – GNU Project – Free Software Foundation (FSF)," http://www.fsf.org/fsf/fsf.html, June 12, 2002.

[84] Friedman, M.A.; Voas, J.M., *Software Assessment: Reliability, Safety, Testability*, New York: John Wiley & Sons, Inc., 1995.

[85] Gabow, H.; Maheshwari, S.N.; Osterwell, L.J., "On two problems in the generation of program test paths," *IEEE Transactions on Software Engineering*, vol. 2 no. 3, September 1976, pp. 227-231.

[86] Gemoets, L.; Kreinovich, V.; Melendez, H., "When to stop testing software? A fuzzy interval approach," in *Proceedings, NAFIPS/IFIS/NASA '94*, San Antonio, TX, USA, December 18-21, 1994, pp. 182-186.

[87] Goel, A.L., "Software reliability models: assumptions, limitations, and applicability," *IEEE Transactions on Software Engineering*, vol. 11 no. 12, Dec. 1985, pp. 1411-1423.

[88] Goel, A.L.; Okumoto, K., "Time-dependent error-detection rate model for software reliability and other performance measures," *IEEE Transactions on Reliability*, vol. 28 no. 3, August 1979, pp. 206-211.

[89] Gotlieb, A.; Botella, B.; Rueher, M., "Automatic test data generation using constraint solving techniques," *Proceedings, ISSTA'98 – International Symposium*

*on Software Testing and Analysis*, Clearwater Beach, FL, USA, March 2-5, 1998, pp. 53-62.

[90] Gorzalczany, M.B., Computational Intelligence Systems and Applications: Neuro-Fuzzy and Fuzzy Neural Synergisms, New York: Physica-Verlag Heidelberg, 2002.

[91] Goyal, A.; Sankar, S., "The application of formal specifications to software documentation and debugging," in *Proceedings, 1ˢᵗ International Workshop on Automated and Algorithmic Debugging*, Linkeoping, Sweden, May 3-5, 1993, pp. 333-349.

[92] Grant, E.L.; Leavenworth, R.S., *Statistical Quality Control, 7ᵗʰ Ed.*, New York: McGraw-Hill, 1996.

[93] Gray, A.R., "A simulation-based comparison of empirical modeling techniques for software metric models of development effort," in *Proceedings of the 6ᵗʰ International Conference on Neural Information Processing*, 1999, pp. 526-531.

[94] Gray, A.R.; MacDonell, S.G., "A comparison of techniques for developing predictive models of software metrics," *Information and Software Technology*, vol. 39, 1997, pp. 425-437.

[95] Gray, A; MacDonell, S., "Applications of Fuzzy Logic to Software Metric Models for Development Effort Estimation," *Proceedings of the Annual Meeting of the North American Fuzzy Information Processing Society -- NAFIPS*, Syracuse, NY, USA, September 21-24, 1997, pp. 394-399.

[96] Gray, A.R.; MacDonell, S.G., "Fuzzy logic for software metric models throughout the development life-cycle," in *Proceedings, 18ᵗʰ International Conference of the North American Fuzzy Information Processing Society – NAFIPS*, New York, NY, USA, June 10-12, 1999, pp. 258-262.

[97] Halstead, M., *Elements of Software Science*, New York: Elsevier, 1977.

[98] Hamlet, D.; Taylor, R., "Partition testing does not inspire confidence," *IEEE Transactions on Software Engineering*, vol. 16 no. 12, December 1990, pp. 1402-1411.

[99] Hausen, H.L., "Knowledge based invocation of software methods and tools," in *Proceedings, 1ˢᵗ IEEE International Workshop on Tools for Artificial Intelligence*, Fairfax, VA, USA, Oct. 23-25, 1989, pp. 499-510.

[100] Hayes-Roth, B.; Pfleger, K.; Lalanda, P.; Morignot, P.; Balabanovic, M., "A domain-specific software architecture for adaptive intelligent systems," *IEEE Transactions on Software Engineering*, vol. 21 no. 4, April 1995, pp. 288-301.

[101] Haykin, S., *Neural Networks: A Comprehensive Foundation, 2ⁿᵈ Ed.*, Upper Saddle River, NJ: Prentice Hall, 1999.

[102] Hebb, D.O., The Organization of Behavior: A Neuropsychological Theory, New York: John Wiley & Sons, 1949.

[103] Hegger, R.; Kantz, H.; Schreiber, T., "Practical implementation of nonlinear time series methods: The TISEAN package," *CHAOS* vol. 9 no. 2, 1999, pp. 413-435.

[104] The Hillside Group, "Welcome to the Hillside Group Web Pages," http://hillside.net, August 7, 2002.

[105] Highsmith, J.; Cockburn, A., "Agile software development: the business of innovation," *IEEE Computer*, vol. 34 no. 9, September 2001, pp.120-122.

[106] Ho, D.W.C.; Zhang, P.-A.; Xu, J., "Fuzzy wavelet networks for function learning," *IEEE Transactions on Fuzzy Systems*, vol. 9 no. 1, February 2001, pp. 200-211.

[107] Hoare, C.A.R., "Communicating sequential processes," *Communications of the ACM*, vol. 21 no. 8, August 1978, pp. 666-677.

[108] Holland, J.H., *Adaptation in Natural and Artificial Systems*, Ann Arbor, MI: University of Michigan Press, 1975.

[109] Holland, J.H., *Adaptation in Natural and Artificial Systems*, Cambridge, MA: MIT Press, 1992.

[110] Hoppner, F.; Klawonn, F.; Kruse, R.; Runkler, T., *Fuzzy Cluster Analysis: Methods for Classification, Data Analysis and Image Recognition*, New York: John Wiley & Sons, Inc., 1999.

[111] Horigome, M.; Singpurwalla, N.D.; Soyer, R., "A Bayes empirical Bayes approach for (software) reliability growth," in *Proceedings, Computer Science and Statistics: The 16$^{th}$ Symposium on the Interface*, March 1984, Atlanta, GA, USA, pp. 47-55.

[112] Huang, C.-Y.; Kuo,S.-Y. "Analysis of incorporating logistic testing-effort function into software reliability modeling," *IEEE Transactions on Reliability*, vol. 51 no. 3, September 2002.

[113] IBM Corp., "Multi-Dimensional Separation of Concerns: Software Engineering using Hyperspaces," http://www.research.ibm.com/hyperspace/, 2002.

[114] Iyer, R.K.; Rossetti, D.J., "Effect of system workload on operating system reliability: a study on IBM 3081," *IEEE Transactions on Software Engineering*, vol. 11 no. 12, Dec. 1985, pp. 1438-1448.

[115] Jang, J.-S.R., "ANFIS: adaptive network-based fuzzy inference system," *IEEE Transactions on Systems, Man and Cybernetics*, vol. 23 no. 3, May 1993, pp. 665-685.

[116] Jang, J.-S.R.; Sun, C.-T.; Mizutani, E., *Neuro-Fuzzy and Soft Computing: A Computational Approach to Learning and Machine Intelligence*, Upper Saddle River, NJ: Prentice-Hall, Inc., 1997.

[117] Jelinski, Z.; Moranda, P.B., "Software reliability research," in *Proceedings, Statistical Computer Performance Evaluation*, November 22-23, 1971, Providence, RI, USA, pp. 465-484.

[118] Jensen, H.A.; Vairavan, K., "An Experimental Study of Software Metrics for Real-Time Software," *IEEE Transactions on Software Engineering*, vol. 11, no. 2, Feb. 1985, pp. 231-234.

[119] Jewell, W.S., "Bayesian extensions to a basic model of software reliability," *IEEE Transactions on Software Engineering*, vol. 11 no. 12, Dec. 1985, pp. 1465-1471.

[120] Jones, C.B., *Systematic Software Development Using VDM*, Englewood Cliffs, NJ: Prentice Hall, 1989.

[121] Jones, C., *Software Quality: Analysis and Guidelines for Success*, New York: International Thompson Computer Press, 1997.

[122] Jones, C., Software Assessments, Benchmarks, and Best Practices, New York: Addison-Wesley, 2000.

[123] Jones, W.D; Vouk, M.A., "Field data analysis," in Lyu, M.R., Ed., *Handbook of Software Reliability Engineering,* New York: McGraw-Hill, 1996, pp. 439-489.

[124] Joyce, D.T., "Examining the potential of fuzzy software requirements specifications," *Information Sciences*, vol. 2, 1994, pp. 85-102.

[125] Kaindl, H., "Object-oriented approaches in software engineering and artificial intelligence," *Journal of Object-Oriented Programming*, vol. 6 no. 8, January 1994, pp. 38-45.

[126] Kan, S.H., *Metrics and Models in Software Quality Engineering*, Reading, MA: Addison-Wesley Pub. Co., 1995.

[127] Kandel, A.; Lee, S.C., *Fuzzy Switching and Automata: Theory and Applications*, New York: Crane, Russak & Company, Inc., 1979.

[128] Kanoun, K.; de Bastos Martini, M.R.; de Souza, J.M., "A method for software reliability analysis and predicition application to the TROPICO-R switching system," *IEEE Transactions on Software Engineering*, vol. 17 no. 4, April 1991, pp. 334-344.

[129] Kant, E., "Understanding and automating algorithm design," *IEEE Transactions on Software Engineering*, vol. 11 no. 11, November 1985, pp. 1361-1374.

[130] Kantz, H.; Schreiber, T., *Nonlinear Time Series Analysis,* New York: Cambridge University Press, 1997.

[131] Kapur, D., "An automated tool for analyzing completeness of equational specifications," *Proceedings, ISSTA '94 – International Symposium on Software Testing and Analysis*, Seattle, WA, USA, Aug. 17-19, 1994, pp. 28-43.

[132] Karunanithi, N.; Whitley, D., "Prediction of software reliability using feedforward and recurrent neural nets," in *Proceedings IJCNN, International Joint Conference on Neural Networks*, June 7-11, 1992, Baltimore, MD, USA, pp. 800-805.

[133] Karunanithi, N.; Malaiya, Y.K., "Neural networks for software reliability engineering," in M.R. Lyu, Ed., *Handbook of Software Reliability Engineering*, New York: McGraw-Hill, 1996, pp. 699-728.

[134] Keiller, P.A.; Littlewood, B.; Miller, D.R.; Sofer, A., "Comparison of software reliability predictions," *Proceedings, 13th International Symposium on Fault-Tolerant Computing*, June 28-30, 1983, Milano, Italy, pp. 128-134.

[135] Keller, J.M.; Gray, M.R.; Givens, J.A., Jr., "A Fuzzy K-Nearest Neighbor Algorithm," *IEEE Transactions on Systems, Man and Cybernetics*, vol. 15 no. 4, Jul/Aug 1985, pp. 580-585. Reprinted in Bezdek, J.C.; Pal, S.K. *Fuzzy Models for Pattern Recognition: Methods that Search for Structures in Data*, Piscataway, NJ: IEEE Press, 1992, pp. 258-263.

[136] Keller, J.M.; Hunt, D.J., "Incorporating fuzzy membership functions into the Perceptron algorithm," *IEEE Transactions on Pattern Analysis and Machine Intelligence*, vol. 7 no. 6, November 1985, pp. 693-699.

[137] Kernel.Org Organization, Inc., "The Linux Kernel Archives," http://www.kernel.org, August 3, 2002.

[138] Khoshgoftaar, T.M.; Allen, E.B., "Neural networks for software quality prediction," in W. Pedrycz, J.F. Peters, Eds., *Computational Intelligence in Software Engineering*, River Edge, NJ: World Scientific, 1998, pp. 33-63.

[139] Khoshgoftaar, T.M.; Allen, E.B.; Jones, W.D.; Hudepohl, J.P., "Data Mining for Predictors of Software Quality," *International Journal of Software Engineering and Knowledge Engineering*, vol. 9 no. 5, 1999, pp. 547-563.

[140] Khoshgoftaar, T.M.; Allen, E.B.; Jones, W.D.; Hudepohl, J.P., "Classification-tree models of software-quality over multiple releases," *IEEE Transactions on Reliability*, vol. 49 no. 1, March 2000, pp. 4-11.

[141] Khoshgoftaar, T.M.; Evett, M.P.; Allen, E.B.; Chien, P.-D., "An application of genetic programming to software quality prediction," in Pedrycz, W.; Peters, J.F., Eds., *Computational Intelligence in Software Engineering*, River Edge, NJ: World Scientific, 1998, pp. 176-195.

[142] Khoshgoftaar, T.M.; Szabo, R.M., "Investigating ARIMA models of software system quality," *Software Quality Journal*, vol. 4 no. 1, March 1995, pp. 33-48.

[143] Khoshgoftaar, T.M.; Szabo, R.M., "Using Neural Networks to Predict Software Faults During Testing," *IEEE Transactions on Reliability*, vol. 45 no. 3, Sept. 1996, pp. 456-462.

[144] Kim, S.-H.; Jang, C.-W.; Chai, C.-H.; Choi, H.-G., "Trajectory control of robotic manipulators using chaotic neural networks," in *Proceedings, ICNN'97 – International Conference on Neural Networks*, Houston, TX, USA, June 9-12, 1997, pp. 1685-1688.

[145] King, K.N.; Offutt, A.J., "A Fortran language system for mutation-based software testing," *Software-Practice and Experience*, vol. 21 no. 7, July 1991, pp. 685-718.

[146] Klir, G.J; Yuan, B., *Fuzzy Sets and Fuzzy Logic: Theory and Applications*, Upper Saddle River, NJ: Prentice Hall PTR, 1995.

[147] Korel, B., "Automated software test data generation," *IEEE Transactions on Software Engineering*, vol. 16 no. 8, August 1990, pp. 870-879.

[148] Korel, B., "Automated test data generation for programs with procedures," in *Proceedings, ISSTA'96 – International Symposium on Software Testing and Analysis*, San Diego, CA, USA, Jan. 8-10, 1996, pp. 209-215.

[149] Korel, B.; Yalamanchili, S., "Forward computation of dynamic program slices," in *Proceedings, ISSTA'94 – International Symposium on Software Testing and Analysis*, Seattle, WA, USA, Aug. 17-19, 1994, pp. 66-79.

[150] Kubat, M.; Matwin, S., "Addressing the curse of imbalanced training sets: one-sided selection," in *Proceedings, 14th Int. Conf. On Machine Learning*, Nashville, TN, USA, July 8-12, 1997, pp. 179-186.

[151] Kyparisis, J.; Singpurwalla, N.D., "Bayesian inference for the Weibull process with applications to assessing software reliability growth and predicting software failures," in *Proceedings, Computer Science and Statistics: The 16th Symposium on the Interface*, March 1984, Atlanta, GA, USA, pp. 57-64.

[152] Laprie, J.-C.; Kanoun, K., "Software Reliability and System Reliability," in Lyu, M.R., Ed., *Handbook of Software Reliability Engineering*, New York: McGraw-Hill, 1996, pp. 27-68.

[153] Laprie, J.-C.; Kanoun, K.; Beounes, C.; Kaaniche, M., "The KAT (Knowledge-Action-Transformation) approach to the modeling and evaluation of reliability and availability growth," *IEEE Transactions on Software Engineering*, vol. 17 no. 4, April 1991, pp. 370-382.

[154] Laski, J.W.; Korel, B., "A data flow oriented program testing strategy," *IEEE Transactions on Software Engineering*, vol. 9 no. 3, May 1983, pp. 347-354.

[155] Last, M., "Info-Fuzzy Network (IFN)," http://www.ise.bgu.ac.il/faculty/mlast/ifn.htm, October 25, 2001.

[156] Last, M.; Kandel, A., "Data Mining for Process and Quality Control in the Semiconductor Industry", *Data Mining for Design and Manufacturing: Methods and Applications*, D. Braha (ed.), Kluwer Academic Publishers, pp. 207-234, 2001.

[157] Last, M.; Maimon, O.; Kandel, A., "Knowledge Discovery in Mortality Records: An Info-Fuzzy Approach", in *Medical Data Mining and Knowledge Discovery*, K. Cios (Ed.), *Studies in Fuzziness and Soft Computing*, Vol. 60, Springer-Verlag, pp. 211-235, 2001.

[158] Lee, S.C.; Lee, E.T., "Fuzzy sets and neural networks," *Journal of Cybernetics*, vol. 4 no. 2, 1974, pp. 83-103.

[159] Lee, S.C.; Lee, E.T., "Fuzzy neural networks," *Mathematical Biosciences*, vol. 23, 1975, pp. 151-177.

[160] Lehman, M.M., "Software Evolution," in Marciniak, J.J., Ed., *Encyclopedia of Software Engineering*, New York: John Wiley & Sons, Inc., 2002, pp. 1507-1513.

[161] Lewis, D.D.; Catlett, J., "Heterogeneous uncertainty sampling for supervised learning," in *Proceedings 11th Int. Conf. On Machine Learning*, Rutgers University, New Brunswick, NJ, USA, July 10-13, 1994, pp. 148-156.

[162] Lewis, E.E., *Introduction to Reliability Engineering, 2nd Ed.*, New York: John Wiley & Sons, Inc., 1996.

[163] Liang, Q.; Mendel, J.M., "Interval type-2 fuzzy logic systems: theory and design," *IEEE Transactions on Fuzzy Systems*, vol. 8 no. 5, October 2000, pp. 535-550.

[164] Lieberherr, K.J., "Demeter / Center for Software Sciences," http://www.ccs.neu.edu/research/demeter/, August 9, 2002.

[165] Lieberman, H., "The debugging scandal and what to do about it," *Communications of the ACM*, vol. 40 no. 4, April 1997, pp. 26-29.

[166] Lind, R.K,"An Experimental Study of Software Metrics and Their Relationship to Software Errors," Master's Thesis, University of Wisconsin-Milwaukee, 1986.

[167] Lind, R.K.; Vairavan, K., "An Experimental Investigation of Software Metrics and Their Relationship to Software Development Effort," *IEEE Transactions on Software Engineering*, vol. 15 no. 5, May 1989, pp. 649-653.

[168] Lindholm, T.; Yellin, F., *The Java™ Virtual Machine Specification*, Palo Alto, CA: Sun Microsystems, Inc., 1999.

[169] Lions, J.L., "Ariane-5 flight 501 failure: report by the inquiry board," http://java.sun.com/people/jag/Ariane5.html, July 19, 1996.

[170] Littlewood, B., "Software reliability model for modular program structure," *IEEE Transactions on Reliability*, vol. 28 no. 3, Aug. 1979, pp. 241-246.

[171] Littlewood, B., "Theories of software reliability: how good are they and how can they be improved?" *IEEE Transactions on Software Engineering*, vol. 6 no. 5, Sept. 1980, pp. 489-500.

[172] Littlewood, B.; Verrall, J.L., "A Bayesian reliability model with a stochastically monotone failure rate," *IEEE Transactions on Reliability*, vol. 23 no. 2, June 1974, pp. 108-114.

[173] Loomis, M.E.S.; Loomis, T.P., "Prototyping and artificial intelligence," in *Prototyping*, New York: Pergamon Infotech, 1986.

[174] Lyu, M.R., Ed., *Handbook of Software Reliability Engineering*, New York: McGraw-Hill, 1996.

[175] Lyu, M.R., "Data and Tool Disk," in Lyu, M.R., Ed., *Hadbook of Software Reliability Engineering,* New York: McGraw-Hill, 1996.

[176] Maimon, O.; Last, M., Knowledge Discovery and Data Mining: The Info-Fuzzy Network (IFN) Methodology, New York: Kluwer Academic Pub., 2000.

[177] Mamdani, E.H., "Application of fuzzy algorithm for control of simple dynamic plant," *Proceedings of the Institute of Electrical Engineers*, vol. 121, 1974, pp. 1585-1588.

[178] Mandelbrot, B.B., *The Fractal Geometry of Nature*, San Francisco, CA: W.H. Freeman, 1983.

[179] von Mayrhauser, A.; France, R.; Scheetz, M.; Dahlman, E., "Generating test cases from an object-oriented model with an artificial-intelligence planning system," *IEEE Transactions on Reliability*, vol. 49 no. 1, March 2000, pp. 26-36.

[180] Mazzuchi, T.A.; Soyer, R., "A Bayes-empirical Bayes model for software reliability," *IEEE Transactions on Reliability*, vol. 37 no. 2, June 1988, pp. 248-254.

[181] McCabe, T.J., "A Complexity Measure," *IEEE Transactions on Software Engineering*, vol. 2 no. 4, Dec. 1976, pp. 308-320.

[182] McCulloch, W.S.; Pitts, W., "A logical calculus of the ideas immanent in nervous activity," *Bulletin of Mathematical Biophysics*, vol. 5, 1943, pp. 115-133.

[183] McDermid, J.A., *Software Engineer's Reference Book*, Oxford, U.K.: Butterworth-Heinemann Ltd., 1991.

[184] McLellan, S.; Roesler, A.; Fei, Z.; Chandran, S.; Spinuzzi, C., "Experience using web-based shotgun measures for large-system characterization and improvement,"

*IEEE Transactions on Software Engineering*, vol. 24 no. 4, April 1998, pp. 268-277.

[185] Memon, A.F., *A Comprehensive Framework for Testing Graphical User Interfaces*, Ph.D. Dissertation, University of Pittsburgh, 2001.

[186] Memon, A.F., "GUI testing: pitfalls and process," *IEEE Computer,* vol. 35 no. 8, August 2002, pp. 87-88.

[187] Mendel, J.M.; Jordan, R.I.B., "Type-2 fuzzy sets made simple," *IEEE Transactions on Fuzzy Systems,* vol. 10 no. 2, April 2002, pp. 117-127.

[188] Mendonca, M.G.; Basili, V.R.; Bhandari, I.S.; Dawson, J., "An approach to improving existing measurement frameworks," *IBM Systems Journal*, vol. 37 no. 4, 1998, pp. 484-501.

[189] Mendonca, M.G.; Basili, V.R., "Validation of an approach for improving existing measurement frameworks," *IEEE Transactions on Software Engineering*, vol. 26 no. 6, June 2000, pp. 484-499.

[190] Mertoguno, J.S.; Paul, R,; Bourbakis, N.G.; Ramamoorthy, C.V., "A Neuro-Expert System for the Prediction of Software Metrics," *Engineering Applications of Artificial Intelligence*, vol. 9 no. 2, 1996, pp. 153-161.

[191] Michael, C.C.; Jones, R.C., "On the uniformity of error propagation in software," in *Proceedings, COMPASS'97*, Gaithersburg, MD, USA, June 16-19, 1997, pp. 68-76.

[192] Michael, C.; McGraw, G., "Automated software test data generation for complex programs," in *Proceedings, 13$^{th}$ IEEE International Conference on Automated Software Engineering*, Honolulu, HI, USA, Oct. 13-16, 1998, pp. 136-146.

[193] Michael, C.C.; McGraw, G.; Schatz, M.A., "Generating software test data by evolution," *IEEE Transactions on Software Engineering*, vol. 27 no. 12, December 2001, pp. 1085-1110.

[194] Microsoft, Inc., "August 2002, Cumulative Patch for Internet Explorer," http://www.microsoft.com/windows/ie/downloads/critical/q323759ie/default.asp, August 22, 2002.

[195] Miller, D.R., "Exponential order statistic models of software reliability growth," *IEEE Transactions on Software Engineering*, vol. 12 no. 1, Jan. 1986, pp. 12-24.

[196] Miller, E.F., Jr., "Program testing: guest editor's introduction," *IEEE Computer*, vol. 11 no. 4, April 1978, pp. 10-12.

[197] Miller, S.K., "Aspect-oriented programming takes aim at software complexity," *IEEE Computer*, vol. 34 no. 4, April 2001, pp. 18-21.

[198] Miller, W.; Spooner, D.L., "Automatic generation of floating-point test data," *IEEE Transactions on Software Engineering*, vol. 2 no. 3, September 1976, pp. 223-226.

[199] Minsky, M.; Papert, S., *Perceptrons: An Introduction to Computational Geometry*, Cambridge, MA: MIT Press, 1969.

[200] Mladenic, D.; Grobelnik, M., "Feature selection for unbalanced class distribution and naïve Bayes," in *Proceedings, 16ᵗʰ Int. Conf. On Machine Learning,* Bled, Slovenia, June 27-30, 1999, pp. 258-267.

[201] Mockus, A.; Fielding, R.T; Herbsleb, J.D., "Two case studies of open source software development: Apache and Mozilla," *ACM Transactions on Software Engineering and Methodology*, vol. 11 no. 3, July 2002, pp. 309-346.

[202] Moranda, P.B., "Event-altered rate models for general reliability analysis," *IEEE Transactions on Reliability*, vol. 28 no. 5, Dec. 1979, pp. 376-381.

[203] Morell, L.; Murrill, B., "Perturbation analysis of computer programs," in *Proceedings, COMPASS'97,* Gaithersburg, MD, USA, June 16-19, 1997, pp. 77-87.

[204] Mostow, J., "Foreword: what is AI? And what does it have to do with software engineering?" *IEEE Transactions on Software Engineering*, vol. 11 no. 11, November 1985, pp. 1253-1256.

[205] Munson, J.C.; Khoshgoftaar, T.M., "Software Metrics for Reliability Assessment," in M.R. Lyu, Ed., *Handbook of Software Reliability Engineering*, New York: McGraw-Hill, 1996.

[206] Musa, J.D., "Validity of execution-time theory of software reliability," *IEEE Transactions on Reliability*, vol. 28 no. 3, August 1979, pp. 181-191.

[207] Musa, J; Fuoco, G.; Irving, N.; Kropfl, D.; Juhlin, B., "The operational profile," in Lyu, M.R., Ed., *Handbook of Software Reliability Engineering,* New York: McGraw-Hill, 1996, pp. 167-254.

[208] Musa, J.D.; Okomuto, K., "Software reliability models: concepts, classification, comparisons, and practice," in Skwirzynski, J.K., Ed., *Electronic Systems Effectiveness and Life Cycle Costing*, Heidelberg: Springer-Verlag, 1983, pp. 395-424.

[209] Musa, J.D.; Okumoto, K., "A logarithmic Poisson execution time model for software reliability measurement," in *Proceedings of the 7ᵗʰ International Conference on Software Engineering*, March 26-29, 1984, Orlando, FL, USA, pp. 230-238.

[210] Natarajan, B.K., *Machine Learning: A Theoretical Approach*, San Mateo, CA: Morgan Kaufmann Pub., Inc., 1991.

[211] Naughton, P.; Schildt, H., *Java: The Complete Reference*, Berkeley, CA: Osborne McGraw-Hill, 1997.

[212] von Neumann, J, "Probabilistic logics and the synthesis of reliable organisms from unreliable components," in *Automata Studies*, Shannon, C.E.; McCarthy, J., Eds., Princeton, NJ: Princeton University Press, 1956, pp. 43-98.

[213] Nourani, C.F., "Multiagent AI implementations and emerging software engineering trend," *Engineering Applications of Artificial Intelligence*, vol. 12, 1999, pp. 37-42.

[214] Ntafos, S.C., "On required element testing," *IEEE Transactions on Software Engineering*, vol. 10 no. 6, November 1984, pp. 795-803.

[215] Offutt, A.J.; Pan, J., "Detecting equivalent mutants and the feasible path problem," in *Proceedings, COMPASS '96: 11th Annual Conference on Computer Assurance*, Gaithersburg, MD, USA, June 17-21, 1996, pp. 224-236.

[216] Offutt, A.J.; Seaman, E.J., "Using symbolic execution to aid automatic test generation," in *Proceedings, COMPASS '90: 5th Annual Conference on Computer Assurance*, Gaithersburg, MD, USA, June 25-28, 1990, pp. 12-21.

[217] Offutt, A.J.; Xiong, Y.; Liu, S., "Criteria for generating specification-based tests," in *Proceedings, ICECCS'99 – IEEE International Conference on Engineering of Complex Computer Systems*, Las Vegas, NV, USA, Oct. 18-21, 1999, pp. 119-129.

[218] Ohba, M., "Software reliability analysis models," *IBM Journal of Research and Development*, vol. 28 no. 4, July 1984, pp. 428-443.

[219] Oivo, M.; Basili, V.R., "Representing software engineering models: the TAME goal-oriented approach," *IEEE Transactions on Software Engineering*, vol. 18 no. 10, October 1992, pp. 886-898.

[220] Okumoto, K., "A statistical method for software quality control," *IEEE Transactions on Software Engineering*, vol. 11 no. 12, Dec. 1985, pp. 1424-1430.

[221] Open Source Initiative, "Open Source Initiative OSI," http://www.opensource.org, 2002.

[222] Pal, S.K.; Mitra, S., "Multilayer perceptron, fuzzy sets, and classification," *IEEE Transactions on Neural Networks*, vol. 3 no. 5, September 1992, pp. 683-697.

[223] Pal, S.K.; Mitra, S., *Neuro-Fuzzy Pattern Recognition Methods in Soft Computing*, New York: John Wiley & Sons, Inc., 1999.

[224] Palo Alto Research Center, Inc., "AspectJ – Apsect-Oriented Programming (AOP) for Java," http://www.aspectj.org, July 24, 2002.

[225] Pargas, R.P.; Harrold, M.J.; Peck, R.R., "Test-data generation using genetic algorithms," *Software Testing, Verification and Reliability*, vol. 9 no. 4, Dec. 1999, pp. 263-282.

[226] Paul, R.A.; Kunii, T.L.; Shinagawa, Y.; Khan, M.F., "Software metrics knowledge and databases for project management," *IEEE Transactions on Knowledge and Data Engineering*, vol. 11 no. 1, Jan./Feb. 1999, pp. 255-264.

[227] Paulk, M.C.; Curtis, B.; Chrissis, M.B.; Weber, C.V., "Capability Maturity Model, Version 1.1," *IEEE Software*, vol. 10 no. 4, July 1993, pp. 18-27.

[228] Pazzani, M.; Merz, C.; Murphy, P.; Ali, K.; Hume, T.; brunk, C., "Reducing misclassification costs," in *Proceedings, 11th Int. Conf. On Machine Learning*, Rutgers University, New Brunswick, NJ, USA, July 10-13, 1994, pp. 217-225.

[229] Pedrycz, W.; Bezdek, J.C.; Hathaway, R.J.; Rogers, G.W., "Two nonparametric models for fusing heterogeneous fuzzy data," *IEEE Transactions on Fuzzy Systems*, vol. 6 no. 3, August 1998, pp. 411-425.

[230] Pedrycz, W.; Peters, J.F.; Ramanna, S., "Design of a software quality decision system: a computational intelligence approach," in *Proceedings, IEEE Canadian Conference on Electrical and Computer Engineering*, Waterloo, ON, Canada, May 24-28, 1998, pp. 513-516.

[231] Pedrycz, W.; Smith, M.H., "Granular Correlation Analysis in Data Mining," in Proceedings of the 18th International Conference of the North American Fuzzy Information Processing Society – NAFIPS, 1999, pp. 715 – 719.

[232] Peters, J.F.; Pedrycz, W., *Software Engineering: An Engineering Approach*, New York: John Wiley & Sons, 2000.

[233] Peters, J.F.; Han, L.; Ramanna, S., "Approximate time rough software cost decision system: multicriteria decision-making approach," in Ras, Z.W. and Skowron, A. (Eds.), *Foundations of Intelligent Systems, Lecture Notes in Artificial Intelligence 1609*. Berlin, Germany: Springer Verlag, 1999, pp. 556-564.

[234] Peterson, J.L., *Petri Net Theory and the Modeling of Systems*, Englewood Cliffs, NJ: Prentice Hall, 1981.

[235] Pham, H.; Nordmann, L.; Zhang, X., "A general imperfect-software-debugging model with S-shaped fault-detection rate," *IEEE Transactions on Reliability*, vol. 48 no. 2, June 1999, pp. 169-175.

[236] Pham, H.; Wang, H., "A quasi-renewal process for software reliability and testing costs," *IEEE Transactions on Systems, Man and Cybernetics, Part A: Systems and Humans*, vol. 31 no. 6, Nov. 2001, pp. 623-631.

[237] Pham, L.; Pham, H., "Software reliability models with time-dependent hazard function based on Bayesian approach," *IEEE Transactions on Systems, Man and Cybernetics – Part A: Systems and Humans*, vol. 30 no. 1, January 2000, pp. 25-35.

[238] Pham, L.; Pham, H., "A Bayesian predictive software reliability model with pseudo-failures," *IEEE Transactions on Systems, man & Cybernetics – Part A: Systems and Humans*, vol. 31 no. 3, May 2001, pp. 233-238.

[239] Pillai, K., "The fountain model and its impact on project schedule," *Software Engineering Notes*, vol. 21 no. 2, March 1996, pp. 32-38.

[240] Prasanna Kumar, V.K.; Hariri, S.; Raghavendra, C.S.; "Distributed program reliability analysis," *IEEE Transactions on Software Engineering*, vol. 12 no. 1, Jan. 1986, pp. 42-50.

[241] Prechelt, L.; Unger, B.; Tichy, W.F.; Brossler, P.; Votta, L.G., "A controlled experiment in maintenance comparing design patterns to simpler solutions," *IEEE Transactions on Software Engineering*, vol. 27 no.12, December 2001, pp. 1134-1144.

[242] Provenzale, A.; Smith, L.A.; Vio, R.; Murante, G., "Distinguishing between low-dimensional dynamics and randomness in measured time series," Physica D vol. 53, 1992, pp. 31-49.

[243] Provost, F.; Fawcett, T.; Kohavi, R., "The case against accuracy estimation for comparing induction algorithms," in *Proceedings, 15th Int. Conf. On Machine Learning,* Madison, WI, USA, July 24-27, 1998, pp. 445-453.

[244] Qiao, H.; Tsokos, C.P., "Estimation of the three parameter Weibull probability distribution," *Mathematics and Computers in Simulation*, vol. 39, 1995, pp. 173-185.

[245] Quinlan, J.R., *C4.5 : programs for machine learning*, San Mateo, CA: Morgan Kaufmann Pub., 1993.

[246] Rajapakse, A.; Furuta, K.; Kondo, S., "Evolutionary learning of fuzzy controllers and their adaptation through perpetual evolution," *IEEE Transactions on Fuzzy Systems*, vol. 10 no. 3, June 2002, pp. 309-321.

[247] Rapps, S.; Weyuker, E.J., "Selecting software test data using data flow information," *IEEE Transactions on Software Engineering*, vol. 11 no. 4, April 1985, pp. 367-375.

[248] Reynolds, R.G.; Zannoni, E., "Extracting procedural knowledge from software systems using inductive learning in the PM system," *International Journal on Artificial Intelligence Tools*, vol. 1 no. 3, 1992, pp. 351-367.

[249] Rice, J.A., *Mathematical Statistics and Data Analysis*, Belmont, CA: Wadsworth Pub. Co., 1995.

[250] Richardson, D.J.; Clarke, L.A., "Partition analysis: a method combining testing and verification," *IEEE Transactions on Software Engineering*, vol. 11 no. 12, December 1985, pp. 1477-1490.

[251] Roberts, H., *Predicting the Performance of Software Systems via the Power Law Process*, Ph.D. Dissertation, University of South Florida, December 2000.

[252] Rosenblatt, F., "The Perceptron: a probabilistic model for information storage and organization in the brain," *Psychological Review*, vol. 65 no. 6, 1958, pp. 386-408.

[253] Ross, S.M., "Software reliability: the stopping rule problem," *IEEE Transactions on Software Engineering*, vol. 11 no. 12, Dec. 1985, pp. 1472-1476.

[254] Royce, W.W., "Managing the development of large software systems: concepts and techniques," in *Proceedings of Wescon*, Aug. 1970 Reprinted in *Proceedings, 9th International Conference on Software Engineering*, Monterey, CA, USA, March 30-April 2, 1987, pp. 328-338.

[255] Rumelhart, D.E.; Hinton, G.E.; Williams, R.J., "Learning internal representations by error propagation," in *Parallel Distributed Processing: Explorations in the Microstructure of Cognition*, Rumelhart, D.E.; McClelland, J.L., Eds., Cambridge, MA: MIT Press, 1986, pp. 318-362.

[256] Russell, S.; Norvig, P., *Artificial Intelligence: A Modern Approach*, Upper Saddle River, NJ: Prentice-Hall, Inc., 1995.

[257] Russo, M., "FuGeNeSys - A fuzzy genetic neural system for fuzzy modeling," *IEEE Transactions on Fuzzy Systems*, vol. 6 no. 3, August 1998, pp. 373-388.

[258] Ryder, B.G., "Constructing the call graph of a program," *IEEE Transactions on Software Engineering*, vol. 5 no. 3, May 1979, pp. 216-226.

[259] Scheetz, M.; von Mayrhauser, A.; France, R., "Generating test cases from an OO model with an AI planning system," in *Proceedings, International Symposium on Software Reliability Engineering*, Boca Raton, FL, USA, November 1-4, 1999, pp. 250-259.

[260] Schneidewind, N.F., "Analysis of error processes in computer software," *SIGPLAN Notices*, vol. 10 no. 6, 1975, pp. 337-346.

[261] Scholz, F.-W., "Software reliability modeling and analysis," *IEEE Transactions on Software Engineering*, vol. 12 no. 1, Jan. 1986, pp. 25-31.

[262] Schreiber, T.; Schmitz, A., "Surrogate time series," *Physica D,* vol. 142 no. 3-4, Aug. 2000, pp. 346-382.

[263] Schwanke, R.W.; Hanson, S.J., "Using neural networks to modularize software," *Machine Learning*, vol. 15, 1994, pp. 137-168.

[264] Schwenk, H.; Bengio, Y., "AdaBoosting neural networks: application to on-line character recognition," in *Proceedings of ICANN '97*, Lausanne, Switzerland, Oct. 8-10, 1997, pp. 967-972.

[265] Sedigh-Ali, S.; Ghafoor, A.; Paul, R.A., "Software engineering metrics for COTS-based systems," *IEEE Computer,* vol. 35 no. 5, May 2001, pp. 44-50.

[266] Shin, M.; Goel, A.L., "Knowledge Discovery and Validation in Software Metrics Databases," *Proceedings of SPIE - The International Society for Optical Engineering*, vol. 3695, April 1999, pp. 226-233.

[267] Singpurwalla, N.D., "Determining an optimal time interval for testing and debugging software," *IEEE Transactions on Software Engineering,* vol. 17 no. 4, April 1991, pp. 313-319.

[268] Singpurwalla, N.D.; Soyer, R., "Assessing (software) reliability growth using a random coefficient autoregressive process and its ramifications," *IEEE Transactions on Software Engineering*, vol. 11 no. 12, Dec. 1985, pp. 1456-1464.

[269] Smith, D.R.; Kotik, G.B.; Westfold, S.J., "Research on knowledge-based software environments at Kestrel Institute," *IEEE Transactions on Software Engineering*, vol. 11 no. 11, November 1985, pp. 1278-1295.

[270] Sommerville, I., "Artificial intelligence and systems engineering," in Proceedings, AISB'93, 9th Biennial Conference of the Society for the Study of Artificial Intelligence and Simulation of Behavior, Birmingham, U.K., March 29 - April 2, 1993, pp. 48-60.

[271] Spivey, J.M., *The Z Notation: A Reference Manual, 2nd Ed.*, London, UK: Prentice Hall International, 1992.

[272] Srinivasan, K.; Fisher, D., "Machine learning approaches to estimating software development effort," *IEEE Transactions on Software Engineering*, vol. 21 no. 2, February 1995, pp. 126-137.

[273] Steier, D.M.; Kant, E., "The roles of execution and analysis in algorithm design," *IEEE Transactions on Software Engineering*, vol. 11 no. 11, November 1985, pp. 1375-1386.

[274] Stroustrup, B., *The C++ Programming Language, 2nd Ed.*, Reading, MA: Addison-Wesley Pub. Co., 1991.

[275] Stubbs, D.F.; Webre, N.W., *Data Structures with Abstract Data Types and Ada*, Boston, MA: PWS Pub. Co., 1993.

[276] Stumptner, M.; Wotawa, F., "A survey of intelligent debugging," *AI Communications*, vol. 11 no. 1, 1998, pp. 35-51.

[277] Sukert, A.N., "Empirical validation of three software error prediction models," *IEEE Transactions on Reliability*, vol. 28 no. 3, Aug. 1979, pp. 199-205.

[278] Sun Microsystems, Inc., "OpenOffice.org," http://www.openoffice.org/, September 9, 2002.

[279] Takagi, H., "Fusion technology of fuzzy theory and neural networks – survey and future directions," *Proceedings, International Conference on Fuzzy Logic and Neural Networks*, July 1990, Iizuka, Japan, pp. 13-26.

[280] Takagi, T.; Sugeno, M., "Fuzzy identification of systems and its application to modeling and control," *IEEE Transactions on Systems, Man and Cybernetics*, vol. 15, 1985, pp. 116-132.

[281] Tautz, C.; Althoff, K.-D., "Using case-based reasoning for reusing software knowledge," in *Proceedings, 2nd International Conference on Case-Based Reasoning*, Providence, RI, USA, July 25-27, 1997, pp. 156-165.

[282] Tessem, B.; Bjornestad, S., "Analogy and complex software modeling," *Computers in Human Behavior,* vol. 13 no. 4, 1997, pp. 465-486.

[283] Theiler, J.; Eubank, S.; Longtin, A.; Galdrikian, B.; Farmer, J.D., "Testing for nonlinearity in time series: the method of surrogate data," *Physica D*, vol. 58, 1992, pp. 77-94.

[284] Tracey, N.; Clark, J.; Mander, K., "Automated program flaw finding using simulated annealing," in *Proceedings, ISSTA'98 – International Symposium on Software Testing and Analysis*, Clearwater Beach, FL, USA, March 2-5, 1998, pp. 73-81.

[285] Tracey, N.; Clark, J.; Mander, K.; McDermid, J., "Automated test-data generation for exception conditions," *Software – Practice and Experience*, vol. 30, 2000, pp. 61-79.

[286] Turcotte, D.L., *Fractals and Chaos in Geology and Geophysics*, New York: Cambridge University Press, 1992.

[287] Udawatta, L.; Watanabe, K.; Kiguchi, K.; Izumi, K., "Fuzzy-chaos hybrid controller for controlling of nonlinear systems," *IEEE Transactions on Fuzzy Systems*, vol. 10 no. 3, June 2002, pp. 401-411.

[288] Vagoun, T.; Hevner, A., "Feasible input domain partitioning in software testing: RCS case study," *Annals of Software Engineering*, vol. 4, 1997, pp. 159-170.

[289] Vanmali, M.; Last, M.; Kandel, A., "Using a neural network in the software testing process," *International Journal of Intelligent Systems*, vol. 17, 2002, pp. 45-62.

[290] Voas, J.M., "Software testability measurement for assertion placement and fault localization," in *Proceedings, AADEBUG: 2nd International Workshop on Automated and Algorithmic Debugging*, Saint-Malo, France, May 22-24, 1995, pp. 133-144.

[291] Wang, L.-X., *A Course in Fuzzy Systems and Control*, Upper Saddle River, NJ: Prentice Hall PTR, 1997.

[292]  Waters, R.C., "The programmer's apprentice: a session with KBEmacs," *IEEE Transactions on Software Engineering*, vol. 11 no. 11, November 1985, pp. 1296-1320.

[293]  Weiser, M., "Program slicing," *IEEE Transactions on Software Engineering*, vol. 10 no. 4, July 1984, pp. 352-357.

[294]  Werbos, P.J., Beyond Regression: New Tools for Prediction and Analysis in the Behavioral Sciences, Ph.D. Thesis, Harvard University, Cambridge, MA, 1974. Reprinted in The Roots of Backpropagation: From Ordered Derivatives to Neural Networks and Political Forecasting, New York: John Wiley & Sons, 1994.

[295]  Weyuker, E.J.; Jeng, B., "Analyzing partition testing strategies," *IEEE Transactions on Software Engineering*, vol. 17 no. 7, July 1991, pp. 703-711.

[296]  Whittaker, J.A.; Jorgensen, A., "Why software fails," *Software Engineering Notes*, vol. 24 no. 4, July 1999, pp. 81-83.

[297]  Windham, M.P., "Cluster Validity for Fuzzy Clustering Algorithms," *Fuzzy Sets and Systems*, vol. 5 no. 2, 1981, pp. 177-185.

[298]  Wizsoft, Inc., "Wizsoft data mining and text mining: WizRule, WizWhy, WizDoc," http://www.wizsoft.com.

[299]  Xia, G.; Zeephongsekul, P.; Kumar, S., "Optimal software release policies for models incorporating learning in testing," *Asia-Pacific Journal of Operational Research*, vol. 9 no. 2, Nov. 1992, pp. 221-234.

[300]  Xie, X.L.; Beni, G., "A Validity Measure for Fuzzy Clustering," *IEEE Transactions on Pattern Analysis and Machine Intelligence*, vol. 13 no. 8, August 1991, 841-847. Reprinted in Bezdek, J.C.; Pal, S.K., *Fuzzy Models for Pattern Recognition: Methods that Search for Structures in Data*, Piscataway, NJ: IEEE Press, 1992, pp. 219-225.

[301]  Yamada, S.; Ohba, M.; Osaki, S., "S-shaped reliability growth modeling for software error detection," *IEEE Transactions on Reliability*, vol. 32 no. 5, Dec. 1983, pp. 475-478.

[302]  Yamada, S.; Osaki, S., "Software reliability growth modeling: models and assumptions," *IEEE Transactions on Software Engineering*, vol. 11 no. 12, Dec. 1985, pp. 1431-1437.

[303]  Yamaguti, M.; Hata, M.; Kigami, J., *Mathematics of Fractals*, Providence, RI: American Mathematical Society, 1997.

[304]  Yuan, X.; Khoshgoftaar, T.M.; Allen, E.B.; Ganesan, K., "An application of fuzzy clustering to software quality prediction," in *Proceedings of the 3rd IEEE Symposium on Application-Specific Software Engineering Technology*, pp. 85-90, 2000.

[305]  Zadeh, L.A., "Outline of a new approach to the analysis of complex systems and decision processes," *IEEE Transactions on Systems, Man and Cybernetics*, vol. 3 no. 1, Jan. 1973, pp. 28-44.

[306]  Zadeh, L.A., "Fuzzy sets and information granularity," in *Advances in Fuzzy Set Theory and Applications*, Gupta, M.M.; Ragade, R.K.; Yager, R.R., Eds., New

York: North-Holland, 1979. Reprinted in *Fuzzy Sets, Fuzzy Logic, and Fuzzy Systems: Selected Papers by Lotfi A. Zadeh,* Klir, G.J; Yuan, B., Eds., River Edge, NJ: World Scientific Pub. Co., 1996.

[307] Zadeh, L.A., "Fuzzy logic = computing with words," *IEEE Transactions on Fuzzy Systems*, vol. 4 no. 2, May 1996, pp. 103-111.

[308] Zadeh, L.A., "Toward a theory of fuzzy information granulation and its centrality in human reasoning and fuzzy logic," *Fuzzy Sets and Systems*, vol. 90, 1997, pp. 111-127.

[309] Zou, F.-Z.; Li, C.-X., "A chaotic model for software reliability," *Chinese Journal of Computers*, vol. 24 no. 3, 2001, pp. 281-291.

[310] S. Dick, C. Bethel, A. Kandel, "Software reliability modeling: the case for deterministic behavior," submitted to *IEEE Transactions on Systems, Man and Cybernetics, Part A: Systems and Humans.*

# About the Authors

**Scott H. Dick** received a B.Sc. from the University of South Florida in Tampa, FL, in 1997, a M.Sc. from USF in 1999, both in Computer Science, and a Ph.D. in Computer Science & Engineering from USF in 2002. He has been an Assistant Professor in the Department of Electrical and Computer Engineering at the University of Alberta in Edmonton, AB, since August 2002. He served as Publications Chair for the 2004 NAFIPS International Conference, and as the organizing chair for an invited session at the 2001 Joint IFSA World Congress and NAFIPS International Conference. Dr. Dick is a member of the ACM, IEEE, ASEE, and Sigma Xi.

Dr. Dick received an Outstanding Student Paper Award at the 2001 Joint IFSA World Conference and NAFIPS International Conference, and the 2003 University of South Florida Outstanding Dissertation Prize. He is the author of over a dozen research papers in scientific journals and conferences. Dr. Dick's research interests are in computational intelligence, data mining, and software engineering.

**Abraham Kandel** received a B.Sc. from the Technion – Israel Institute of Technology and a M.S. from the University of California, both in Electrical Engineering, and a Ph.D. in Electrical Engineering and Computer Science from the University of New Mexico. Dr. Kandel, a Distinguished University Professor and the Endowed Eminent Scholar in Computer Science and Engineering at the University of South Florida is the Executive Director of the newly established National Institute for Systems Test and Productivity. He was the Chairman of the Computer Science and Engineering Department at the University of South Florida (1991-2003) and the Founding Chairman of the Computer Science Department at Florida State University (1978-1991). He also was the Director of the Institute of Expert Systems and Robotics at FSU and the Director of the State University System Center for Artificial Intelligence at FSU. He is Editor of the *Fuzzy Track—IEEE MICRO*; Area Editor on

Fuzzy Hardware for the International Journal "Fuzzy Sets and Systems," an Associate Editor of the journals *IEEE Transactions on Systems, Man and Cybernetics; Control Engineering Practice; International Journal of Pattern Recognition and Artificial Intelligence,* and a member of the editorial boards of the international journals *International Journal of Expert Systems: Research and Applications; The Journal of Fuzzy Mathematics; IEEE Transactions on Fuzzy Systems; Fuzzy Systems – Reports and Letters; Engineering Applications for Artificial Intelligence; The Journal of Grey Systems; Applied Computing Review Journal (ACR) – ACM; Journal of Neural Network World; Artificial Intelligence Tools; Fuzzy Economic Review; International Journal of Chaotic Systems and Applications; International Journal of Image and Graphics, Pattern Recognition; Book Series on "Studies in Fuzzy Decision and Control;* and *BUSEFAL – Bulletin for Studies and Exchange of Fuzziness and its Applications.*

Dr. Kandel has published over 500 research papers for numerous professional publications in Computer Science and Engineering. He is also the author, co-author, editor or co-editor of 38 textbooks and research monographs in the field. Dr. Kandel is a Fellow of the ACM, Fellow of the IEEE, Fellow of the New York Academy of Sciences, Fellow of AAAS, Fellow of IFSA, as well as a member of NAFIPS, IAPR, ASEE, and Sigma-Xi.

Dr. Kandel has been awarded the College of Engineering Outstanding Research Award, USF, 1993-94; Sigma-Xi Outstanding Faculty Researcher Award, 1995; The Theodore and Venette-Askounes Ashford Distinguished Scholar Award, USF, 1995; MOISIL International Foundation Gold Medal for Lifetime Achievements, 1996; Distinguished Researcher Award, USF, 1997; Professional Excellence Program Award, USF, 1997; Medalist of the Year, Florida Academy of Sciences, 1999; Honorary Scientific Advisor, Romanian Academy of Sciences, 2000.